"Every morning we wake up with an unimpeachable dream to find joy. But sometimes that dream becomes a nightmare: self-secured joy is just a shadow. At the end of a restless day we look to the self-help gurus but they can only give us magnifying glasses to gaze more deeply into our own navels. Lift your sights through *The Joy Project*, and rejoice to read that joy is actually coming *for you*."

—GLORIA FURMAN, author of *Treasuring Christ When Your Hands Are Full*

"Our eyes of flesh seek joy in the wrong places, define it with a bankrupt vocabulary, and settle for it using mistaken formulas. Because we don't know what to do but try harder and hide our shame, we get stuck and sick, depressed and despondent. This dehumanizes us, discourages us, and defeats us. But there is hope! Read *The Joy Project* and you will see the Lord's design in the Gospel to give you eyes of faith to behold that joy only comes through the electing, atoning, and comforting love of our Triune God. This is applied reformed theology at its best."

—ROSARIA BUTTERFIELD, author of *Secret Thoughts of an Unlikely Convert*

"We all want joy and happiness—but they seem such elusive things. We reach for them and fall, we aim and miss. For me that's because I make them dependent on *me*: how I'm doing, how I'm feeling. Tony Reinke shows a far sweeter way, a way to *solid* joy."

—MICHAEL REEVES, author of *Rejoicing in Christ*

The Joy Project

A True Story of Inescapable Happiness

TONY REINKE

To our prayer and financial partners around the world—
the joyful, generous, and beloved colaborers
behind everything we publish at desiringGod.org.

*The Joy Project: A True Story of Inescapable Happiness*

Copyright © 2015 by Tony Reinke

Download this book in three digital formats, free of charge, at desiringGod.org

This book version: 1.8 (October, 2015)

Published by Desiring God
         Post Office Box 2901
         Minneapolis, MN 55402

ISBN: 978-0-9912776-5-0
Cover design: Christopher Tobias, Tobias' Outerwear for Books
eBook design: Josh Pritchard, Gideon House Books
First printing 2015
Printed in the United States of America

Behold my servant, whom I uphold,
    my chosen, in whom my soul delights;
I have put my Spirit upon him.
                Isaiah 42:1

# We Must Have Joy

How much of your life is driven by the desire for joy?

Well, all of it. We know we need joy like we need food and water. How we get joy is something of a mystery, and most of us are content to leave that mystery unsolved. We simply want to experience the joy we desire.

Joy is real, but joy is also elusive. Just when we think we've got a handful of happiness, we watch it run through our fingers and vanish. Where does it go?

For many of us, this quest for joy leads—with terrible irony—to despair. We pursue joy in materialism, and we get stuck in debt. We pursue joy in our children, and gnaw ourselves with worry over their well-being. We pursue marital perfection, and grumble when we find our spouse's faults.

We aim for joy, and we find doubt. Is joy really so mysterious and circumstantial? Is joy poisoned? What if our desire for ultimate joy is *really* just a curse? What if the promise of all-satisfying joy is life's cruelest hoax?

And yet, no matter how hard we are let down, and no matter how hard we fail, we cannot stop looking for joy. It drives us. We don't stop—we can't stop, we won't stop. So we turn to personal discipline and to how-to books, life hacks, and gimmicky life-organization tools, all thinking that our main problem must be a failure of focus.

We conclude that the barriers to abiding joy are the unhealthy choices that clog our lives. The root problem, we think, is that we're stuck in a rut of predictability and laziness, so we must unstick ourselves. We turn to self-improvement. We make new resolutions. We scour the Internet for list-blogs that promise lasting change with easy effort. We buy productivity apps for our phones. We resolve to become more "chill" parents, sexier spouses, better friend-winners, and more purposeful people-influencers. We need to sit less and walk more. We need to sleep more and eat less. We need to get to the gym a few times a week to lose fat and build muscle. We purge fast food, drop the carbs, and fork down more vegetables. We drink more water, less coffee, less soda. We buy organic, fair trade, rBGH-free, gluten-free, free-range. We pay off credit card debt and build our savings. We clip coupons. We invest money in a new retirement plan. We set aside some funds for a future vacation. We clean out the garage. We purge our closets of junk. We buy apps to track our progress and planners to micromanage our days. We commit to staying on top of our e-mails, checking our phones less often, watching less television, visiting the library more, and reading our neglected stacks of books.

We chase a long list of changes to sharpen our daily routines, to tweak our daily habits, and to find our daily joy. It's no surprise that how-to books promising this high-powered life sell by the millions. One such guide is *The Happiness Project: Or, Why I Spent a Year Trying to Sing in the Morning, Clean My Closets, Fight Right, Read Aristotle, and Generally Have More Fun*, the whimsically titled *New York Times* best seller by Gretchen Rubin.

In her book, and others like it, each step of personal discipline promises to bring a mounting list of small changes that snowball into a happy life. The lesson we learn from it all is what Rubin knows well: Increased joy rarely comes by accident. Most of our "joy" appears after strategic planning, goal setting, and self-discipline, or—on some sweet occasions— by a surprise gift from the planning and sacrifices of a spouse or friend. Sometimes joy is sporadic and surprises us out of nowhere. But usually it is the by-product of goals and planning.

## The Project

Yes, joy does hinge on a plan (more on that in a moment). But the premise behind the promise of all this happiness is the problem. For Rubin and other writers, it all hinges on you: *your* structured resolutions, *your* renewed convictions, and *your* decisive discipline. The hitch with books like *The Happiness Project* is that personal joy gets thrown back on you: *your* initiative, *your* planning, *your* work, *your* determination. Happiness can be yours, but only if you earn it. For the go-getters, joy earned at the end of long lists and assignments may be good news. But most of us see these ploys as tedious and trivial, and we grow more depressed, more burdened, and more buried under the acute sense that, somewhere along the line, we flunked life.

If you are like me, you take stock of your disordered life—the cluttered corners, the grubby margins of your days, and the unkempt middle where you do most of your living—and the result is painfully deflating. Rather than increasing your joy, all this introspection breeds regret and self-loathing.

What if all our focus on changing personal patterns misses a much bigger and more important point?

- What if joy goes deeper than the flimsy foundations of organized day planners, thinned-out closets, freshly painted walls, or a perfectly followed gym routine?
- What if joy is not found at the end of a to-do list?
- What if joy is not governed by the personality assigned to us by the lottery of our genetic heritage?
- What if Aristotle, when he said my happiness depends on me, was fundamentally wrong?

To say it another way: What if I told you someone else is more concerned for your joy than you could ever be? What if this person has been planning your joy since before you were born? Would you believe me, or would you write me off as a well-meaning but ignorant religious optimist? If you'll hear me out, I'll help you understand one inescapable path to personal happiness. The joy ahead is no mirage; it is as real as this book in front of you.

This one path to unending joy is called The Joy Project. This project isn't DIY. You cannot start it, you cannot end it, and you cannot fumble it. You can't even hold the lynchpin to keep it all together. The Joy Project is put in capital letters because it's bigger than you and bigger than me. It was designed and orchestrated *for you*, long before the moment when you awoke to discover that your entire life is driven by the endless hunt for happiness.

## The Joy Project

This project will take some time to understand, and it will require us to be painfully honest with ourselves. We must face the reasons for our unhappiness with unshrinking grit. Do we want to know the truth? The truth is that our lives are filled with so much self-doubt and anxiety that we can hardly remember that we were made by God to rule and reign over this world as we image him. If we're being honest, we don't call ourselves royalty. If we're being honest, we call ourselves timid, confused, and insecure. All our self-loathing and self-promoting is a thin veil covering over our frightening conviction that we are nobodies.

We are not the first to look into this mirror of honest reflection. To wrestle with our common plight, a group of Christians in the seventeenth century gathered to bring clarity to these confusions. At their monumental meeting in a town called Dordrecht, they drafted a theological vision that would later be remembered by its unforgettable acronym, TULIP, the Netherland's most famous flower.[1] TULIP is a mnemonic aid to explain the content of God's redeeming work in the Bible. TULIP is short for these five unfolding points:

- TOTAL DEPRAVITY is not just badness, but blindness to beauty and deadness to joy.
- UNCONDITIONAL ELECTION is how God planned, before we existed, to complete our joy in Christ.
- LIMITED ATONEMENT is the assurance that indestructible joy in God is infallibly secured for us by the blood of Jesus.
- IRRESISTIBLE GRACE is the sovereign commitment of God to make sure we hold on to superior delights instead of the false pleasures that will ultimately destroy us.
- PERSEVERANCE OF THE SAINTS is the almighty work of God to keep us, through all affliction and suffering, for an inheritance of pleasures at God's right hand forever.[2]

This precious acronym is a bulb of truth buried deep in the soil of Scripture. My prayer is that it will sprout, grow, and blossom in your heart and mind as the pages of this book unfold. My hope is that

1   Also know as "The Synod of Dort," after the host city, Dordrecht, the synod spanned November 13, 1618 and May 9, 1619. The result was a document called "Canons of Dordrecht," or "Canons of Dort," which was later summarized into TULIP.

2   John Piper, *The Legacy of Sovereign Joy: God's Triumphant Grace in the Lives of Augustine, Luther, and Calvin* (Wheaton, IL: Crossway, 2006), 73. Slightly edited for parallelism. Formatting added.

you will catch a glimpse of its beautiful narrative, because this story reaches back before the dawn of time, stretches forward into the far reaches of eternity, and fills every gap in between. The terms will make more sense as the story unfolds.

We can call it "TULIP," or "the doctrines of grace," or "Reformed theology," or "Augustinianism," or "Calvinism," or, as I will call it in this book, "The Joy Project." The point is simple. God's Joy Project over our lives is not bound by the circumstances of this fallen, joy-smiting planet. God's plan for our joy rests on a foundation deeper than our daily resolutions. It is bigger than our anxieties and fears. It is brighter than our darkest secrets. It searches our hearts and exposes the roots of our passions and redirects us to eternal joys. Most importantly, The Joy Project reveals the heart of God and the infinite joys he is eager to share.

The Joy Project is a story that reminds us we are characters in God's unfolding cosmic story. God has written our joy into a script and what he planned for us we can hardly imagine. The Joy Project is the boldest and subtlest story ever told. It will shock you, then it will bewilder you, and then it will plunge you into an ocean of divine love. It is a drama told in five acts.

## A Story Told and Retold

The Joy Project is the heartbeat of Scripture. Neglect the Bible, and you neglect God's Joy Project, and you neglect your own joy. As we will discover, we were made for joy and our pursuit of joy is essential to our lives and essential to our obedience to God.[3]

These doctrines of grace are not the deep space of Scripture; rather, they are its major constellations: bright, burning signs of God's sovereign and saving activity. The story is so wonderful, so captivating, that it must be told and retold. For centuries, pastors and theologians have taken this sacred tradition and passed it on to new generations of Christians. The Joy Project is bright in the writings of the early church fathers (pastors and theologians such as Augustine) and shines in the Reformed tradition beginning in the sixteenth century (by men like John Calvin). Later it was carried on by the English Puritans (by men such as Thomas Goodwin, John Owen, David Clarkson, and Thomas Boston) and then passed to the American Puritans of the eighteenth century (notably Jonathan Edwards). In the nineteenth century, pulpits still glowed with its message (principally in the booming voice of the prince of preachers, Charles Spurgeon), and it is now entrusted today to modern Calvinists (such as John Piper and to the men and women online at desiringGod.org). All these voices, from history and from our own time, will help us discover the magnificence of God's plan.

Even though church history tells an important story of The Joy Project, the voice of the Script Writer speaks most credibly and conclusively in the pages of the Bible. God has spoken on this subject

---

3   For a sampling of passages where God simply commands his people to be happy in him, see Deut. 28:47; 1 Chron. 16:31, 33; Neh. 8:10; Pss. 32:11; 33:1; 35:9; 40:8, 16; 42:1–2; 63:1, 11; 64:10; 95:1; 97:1, 12; 98:4; 104:34; 105:3; Isa. 41:16; Joel 2:23; Zech. 2:10; 10:7; Rom. 5:2–3, 11; Phil. 3:1; 4:4.

from many different angles to convince us—without a doubt—of the greatest news in the universe: *Our eternal joy will flourish when we are the object of God's sovereign grace.* Nothing about this story is accidental. God purposed all of it (Rom. 9:11). He planned it. We are alive in the script penned by the triune God; the joy shared by the Father, Son, and Holy Spirit now shared with you and me.

The Joy Project is a script. It's the greatest story ever told. And it's deeply personal. And yet the story is not G-rated. It will cause us to face the dark brutality of our world with blunt honesty. And this is where The Joy Project begins, with act one, a deep dive into the chief motive that drives humanity.

Act 1:

# The World's Joy-Tragedy

In his classic book *Mere Christianity*, former atheist C. S. Lewis offers a profound insight into the psychological engine that pulls along the entire train of human experience: "All that we call human history—money, poverty, ambition, war, prostitution, classes, empires, slavery—is the long terrible story of man trying to find something other than God which will make him happy."[1]

Simply put, the driving motive in history is the desire for happiness. All sin, from slavery to prostitution to racism to terrorism to extortion to the sparks that ignite world wars—all are driven by a desire for happiness apart from God.

In one sentence, Lewis jabs a steel dental probe into the raw, unmedicated nerve of atheism. The greatest hazard we face is not *intellectual atheism*—denying that God exists. Our most desperate problem is *affectional atheism*—refusing to believe God is the object of our greatest and most enduring joy. This is the heart of our foolishness. The fool speaks from the depths of his affections and longings and declares: God is irrelevant (Ps. 14:1).

1   C. S. Lewis, *Mere Christianity* (New York: HarperCollins, 2001), 49.

This is the affectional atheism that plagues every heart.

## Atheists to the Core

As the lessons of history show, such heart cancer spreads social decay and eventual ruin. The problem with the world is not the existence of atheism, but rather the wandering of our hearts. If we could see our motives clearly, we would see our sins starkly. We are born with the temptation to seek joy outside of God, and this affliction affects those around us.[2]

What happens when we seek joy without God? We oppress. We step on toes. We wound and offend. In turn, we are assaulted; other self-absorbed atheists seek their own personal happiness at *our expense*. Believe it: If you don't *use* someone first, you'll *get used* soon enough.

Tragically, these selfish desires often attract people to one another, drawing individuals together and leading them to an inevitable collision. We have all watched this play out in the real world. In the search for joy, a single man who idolizes sex is motivated to date. In the pursuit of joy, a single woman who idolizes the attention of men to fund her sense of self-worth is motivated to date. They meet. At first the pleasures seem fulfilling, but they little comprehend how the surface union and fleeting joys mask a maliciousness underneath. For a moment, it costs the man his time, attention, and money. It costs

2 See Ps. 14:1–4; Rom. 3:10–18.

the woman the vulnerability of her body. But there seems to be a warm glow of love, the gratification of personal desires, and the blossom of a permanently satisfying relationship.

But idols are hungry and never satisfied. Eventually the man's eyes are drawn to the woman at the bar and un-drawn from his woman across the table. The man's kindnesses will eventually be exposed for what they are: unheroic and unmanly offerings, spare change from the pocket of his soul. And, appallingly, the woman's body will be cast aside as merely a crude tool to satisfy a man's godless appetite. Beneath this thin veneer of "love" is a relationship between two sinners, two *isolated* sinners, two atheists whose affections are disconnected from God and who use one another in a futile attempt to fill the gap. It will end in war.

## Fight Club

We exploit one another in our pursuit of personal happiness, and we end up with vicious personal conflict. James 4:1–12 helps us understand why this happens by asking us, point-blank: What causes fights and quarrels in our lives? What fuels the flames of anger, bitterness, and wrath in our hearts?

The answer is profound, but it's not complicated. We war against one another because we claw and cry for godless joys. We idolize the pleasures that we think will satisfy our souls—sex, power, wealth, fame, you name it—but we don't get them, they elude our clutches, and so we covet. We use. We get used.

We seek our worth in superiority, and we step on others in the process. We ride emotional highs and plummet on depressive lows because we value our perceived self-worth more than God's design. In our pride, we become enemies of one another because we have become enemies of God. We reject him. He rejects our rebellion. We reject the abundant supplies of God. We become empty, we use others, and we cut each other down. Welcome to the fight club.

The reality is stark, and the problem is universal. Puritan Richard Sibbes sums up our tragic predicament: "Before the heart be changed, our judgment is depraved in regard of our last end; we seek our happiness where it is not to be found."[3] Misplaced affection is the root problem behind all conflict. Preoccupied with the streams, we are blind to the fountain of joy. We will not seek the presence of God. Blind to God's beauty and to his pleasures, we seek to satisfy ourselves with pleasures of the flesh that are too trivial to sustain hungry souls. Feasting only upon creation as the source of joy, our hearts have withered and died. Born with an appetite for the everlasting, we are starved for sustaining joy.

Look around. Everyone is chasing *something*. That's the point of Lewis and James and Sibbes. Whether we know it or admit it, we all chase an *end*. Our *end* is our chief good, the best thing we labor to obtain, that goal for which we will use everything

---

3   Richard Sibbes, *The Complete Works of Richard Sibbes* (Edinburgh, 1862), 1:181. All quotes have been taken from original sources; however, most of the direct quotes in this book drawn from sixteenth- and seventeenth-century sources have been slightly modified in wording and punctuation to enhance readability. –TR

else in this life to reach. *My* "last end" is whatever *I* determine to be my greatest treasure, or whatever I think will make me happiest to have. Sex or attention or independence or power or fame or wealth: each of these ultimate ends exposes the practical atheism of our hearts. So Puritan Richard Baxter can say: "The chief part of man's corruption consists in a wrong chief good, a wrong treasure, a wrong security."[4]

Perceptive students of the human soul know that the question we all must face cuts very deep: What's the *one thing* I cannot live without?

This question demolishes façades and exposes sin. Sin is not merely wrong *doing*; sin is essentially wrong *adoring*. Sin is the fastening of our hearts on any good, treasure, or security in life that replaces the good, treasure, and security of God. This is the chief question of life. This is the chief determination of our joy. This is the misstep that sends us down the rabbit hole, where we find ourselves lost atheists in the core of our being.

## Idols

We will return to this dynamic at various points throughout the story. For now, we must see our native blindness to God's abundant beauty. Our drifting eyes turn from one idol to another, grow wider at every new delicacy, and feast on a buffet of spiritual adultery. John Calvin explains how this works in the

---

4 Richard Baxter, *The Practical Works of the Rev. Richard Baxter* (London, 1830), 7:39. Language slightly edited.

context of spiritual infidelity: "Adulterers by their wandering glances, generate the flames of lust, and so their heart is set on fire" (Ezek. 6:9).[5] The heart is lured by wandering eyes—eye lust (1 Jn. 2:16). Perceptive marketers know how this works. Take any new digital technology (like an innovative phone), float it in the air before our eyes, give us a long look at the shapely aluminum and the flawless glass face, and we will immediately feel lured to it.

Phones are not sinful, but when we ignore the beauty of God we inevitably worship the visible world. What we see around us is what we hunt, and what we hunt fuels the lust for what we long to see. A new technology only breeds new desires for even newer technology. This futile cycle is never broken, because our eyes are never satisfied (Prov. 27:20).

This also explains why idols take many different forms in every century or culture. Idols appear as wood carved into a sacred pole, gold molded into a calf, ivory shaped into a statuette, cardboard printed into a lottery ticket, a glossy magazine cover printed with an airbrushed image of a model, or a piece of metal and glass brought together in an attractive new phone.

The long trajectory of the human predicament is as a rock climber, eyes scanning to find the next visible handhold, groping for something to satisfy our hearts. With each new hold we increase the flame of lust in our hearts, propelling ourselves toward the summit of godless satisfaction. But the summit is

---

5 John Calvin, *Commentary on the First Twenty Chapters of the Book of the Prophet Ezekiel* (Edinburgh, 1849), 231.

false and the climb is futile. The end never arrives because the aim was wrong from the beginning—it was the wrong mountain. And all the while, with each step, we only increase the height from which eventually we will all fall.

But we keep doing it because we don't know any better. We keep turning back to our addictions to find our meaning and value. Over and over we make this tragic mistake. We become idol addicts.

## Idol Addicts

Meet Joelle van Dyne. Joelle is a young woman who hides her face behind a veil. Why she does so, we don't know. Perhaps she was disfigured in a childhood accident, or perhaps, as she claims, her striking beauty casts a powerful spell over the men in her life. But what we do know is that Joelle, hidden behind her veil, is a forceful character, a stunning creation in David Foster Wallace's hefty novel *Infinite Jest*.

Joelle sets out on an ambitious quest to obtain happiness, and apparently her veil protects her in the pursuit. Groping for pleasure, Joelle turns to freebase cocaine and there she finds an explosive experience that, in a moment, "frees and condenses, compresses the whole experience to the implosion of one terrible shattering spike in the graph, an afflated orgasm of the heart that makes her feel, truly, *attractive*, sheltered by limits, deviled and loved, observed and alone and sufficient and female, full, as if watched for an instant by God."[6] In her potent longing, she discovers in cocaine a fleeting experience of meaning, love, and value. But the feeling is a vapor.

Like Joelle's cocaine, our sin addictions are pleasure-hits of hallucination. The form of our addictions may be more socially acceptable: gambling, gaming, eating, shopping, or fishing for praise from our peers. But the lure behind every addiction is the same. We turn to a God substitute to find our joy, our security, our hope, and our approval. We get a moment's gratification, a faint glimmer of what it must feel like to stand in the beautiful presence of God. But such a feeling is a hallucination. Our idols have no hands to embrace us, no eyes to see us, no mouths to assure us, no ears to hear us. Instead, we who have worshiped them become like them: blind, mute, deaf, and powerless. "Coming down" from our euphoric high, we must battle all over again the anxiety, the paranoia, and the grim realization that once again we have not escaped ourselves. We are no more loved. We are no more satisfied. We are only doomed to repeat this episode of self-destruction.

## Our Idols and Our Community

On the one hand, this is a personal tragedy. By sinning we diminish ourselves. Sin distorts our good and idolatry steals our identity. We are always be-

---

6   David Foster Wallace, *Infinite Jest* (New York: Little, Brown, 1996), 235.

coming what we worship.[7] And that means we are always un-becoming our true selves.[8]

This tragic degeneration of ourselves goes almost unnoticed, said Søren Kierkegaard: "The greatest hazard of all, losing the self, can occur very quietly in the world, as if it were nothing at all. No other loss can occur so quietly; any other loss—an arm, a leg, five dollars, a wife, etc.—is sure to be noticed."[9]

Even if we don't feel them, the consequences are real. Our idols misshape our souls like drugs alter the facial features of a meth addict. Unlike a drug-ravaged face, whose degeneration can be captured by time-lapsed photos, we don't see the drastic changes to our souls quite so readily, but this soul-distortion afflicts everyone who follows after the pleasures of sin.

On the other hand, idolatry is never an isolated tragedy. Addictive pleasures corrode our relationships, our families, and our communities. We naïvely think that our hand-sized, personal idols are our private business, when in fact they are the epicenter of a destructive blast of radiation that issues from us through the lives of countless people. The radiation of our idolatry is often invisible except for the scars it leaves. The idols we latch onto (in our search for love, worth, and security) determine how we evaluate and treat others. One modern theologian explains it well:

---

7   See Rom. 1:23; 8:29; 2 Cor. 3:18; Col. 3:10.

8   Think of the haunting portrait of Weston in C. S. Lewis's novel *Perelandra*.

9   Søren Kierkegaard, *The Sickness unto Death: A Christian Psychological Exposition for Upbuilding and Awakening*, vol. 19, Kierkegaard's Writings, ed. Howard V. Hong and Edna H. Hong (Princeton University Press, 1983), 32–33.

*One of the primary laws of human life is that you become like what you worship; what's more, you reflect what you worship not only back to the object itself but also outward to the world around. Those who worship money increasingly define themselves in terms of it and increasingly treat other people as creditors, debtors, partners, or customers rather than as human beings. Those who worship sex define themselves in terms of it (their preferences, their practices, their past histories) and increasingly treat other people as actual or potential sexual objects. Those who worship power define themselves in terms of it and treat other people as either collaborators, competitors, or pawns. These and many other forms of idolatry combine in a thousand ways, all of them damaging to the image-bearing quality of the people concerned and of those whose lives they touch.*[10]

Our idols blind us to the God-given value of other souls. We end up measuring the worth of others by the idols we worship. We idolize those we want to become, and we become so self-absorbed that we can only envy those who seem superior (or seem to be competing with us). We despise ourselves under those we place above us; we pride ourselves over those we place beneath us. We treat others in harsh and inhumane ways. People are nothing more than our collaborators, our competitors, or our pawns.

10  N. T. Wright, *Surprised by Hope: Rethinking Heaven, the Resurrection, and the Mission of the Church* (New York: HarperOne, 2008), 182.

Our hard and cold idols make us hard and cold people. But though we are terribly alone, we all know from experience that this kind of negative, critical spirit spreads from person to person like flames in a dry forest.

Personal idols dehumanize us. They deform us. They pervert our evaluation of others and erode our relationships. The idol of sex leads us to objectify the bodies of the beautiful and to shun the unattractive. The idol of wealth leads us to objectify the wealthy and to shun the frugal. The idol of physical skill leads us to objectify athletes and to shun the gawky. On and on like this we go in our relationships to the people around us. We judge others on the basis of our pantheon of false gods.

If we deceive ourselves, it is only inevitable that we will also deceive others. Our lives are out of order, and this disorder burdens and tempts everyone we touch. Separated from our true selves, we are a mass of confusion. We seek happiness by lying to ourselves, we view the world through the slanted lenses of our own perverted sense of self-worth, and we confuse and trample everyone else along the way. If sin is the poison of our joy, it is also the lethal dose that we toss into the community well.

## Totally Depraved

If we imagine a dead soul groping for satisfaction where lasting pleasure cannot be found, and ruining other lives in the process, then we accurately picture what is called "total depravity." This is the first letter

in the acronym TULIP, the dark first act in the drama
of God's Joy Project.

*Total depravity* does not mean we are all agents of
unmitigated evil. You and I are not Adolf Hitlers who
promote genocide, consign humans to gas cham-
bers, or live by the drumbeat of demonic cruelty. But
in our fallen human nature, we are all corrupted by
evil desires. Our minds, our wills, our affections, our
imaginations—no piece of our identity escapes the
wicked perversity of our fallen race. So while we're
not all wicked despots who throw bodies into a furnace, we do throw the reputations of others into the
furnace of slander. We talk behind people's backs
and defame our neighbors. We take disturbing delight in the failures of others. The depravity that
massacres reputations is the same depravity that
slays bodies. Our anger is easily stoked into hatred
against others, and this anger is nothing less than
embryonic murder.[11] While the scale of the devasta-
tion we cause will differ and vary from the most vio-
lent in this world, we all carry in us the seeds of the
same depravity. And our depravity is inescapable.

As I quoted earlier, John Piper sums up the tragedy like this: "Total depravity is not just badness, but
blindness to beauty and deadness to joy." Our root
problem is not that we break commandments; our
problem is that we ignore God. Ignoring the beauty of God is the essence of total depravity. It's what
makes the depravity so holistic—we cannot begin
to imagine how any real sense of pleasure or joy can

---

11  See Matt. 5:21–22; 1 John 3:15.

be found in our Creator! To us sinners, God is only a boring obstacle to our pleasure. This dynamic is what makes our depravity *total*.

## Guilty Pleasures

Let's turn again to the old Puritans who understood how this sly depravity works. They said that to be dominated by sin is to have the heart's affections "vitiated"—an old way of saying the emotions are mangled beyond recognition. Depravity spoils the heart of what it was created to be and do.

The sinner's plight is this: "He cannot get his wicked will gratified, or his carnal affections satisfied."[12] When the natural world offers no more satisfying delights, the heart lusts for unnatural ones (Rom. 1:18–32). Because the sinner's lusts are insatiable, the sum total of this finite world cannot gratify him.

We are dying sinners in desperate need of a spiritual double bypass surgery, but we spend our pocket change on double cheeseburgers. We get happy again with a momentary food buzz, but the temporary buzz is slowly killing us. This is fundamentally what it means to be a sinner, and our self-undoing sins often go unnoticed because they are socially accepted (and sometimes socially celebrated). Behind all sin is a corrupt heart lusting after not only what ignores God, but ultimately what ruins our joy. We would have it no other way.

12   Ralph Erskine, *The Sermons and Other Practical Works of the Late Reverend and Learned Mr. Ralph Erskine* (Glasgow: W. Smith, 1777), 1:390.

The reality of total depravity lands us here. We love what destroys us; we are blind to what satisfies us. Total depravity suffocates the soul's happiness by the soul's own wayward desires. It is total blindness to God's matchless beauty. It is total resistance to supreme joy in God. It is the essence of all sin. Low thoughts about God are the root of our total depravity. This is the great human tragedy. This is affectional atheism.

Not only are we blind to God, but, in the words of the prophet Jeremiah, we love to have it so (Jer. 5:31). To be totally depraved is to be more than a victim of sin. It's not merely forgetting God, a problem remedied by iPhone alarms or weekly church attendance. Sin is our preference. Depravity is volitional. Sin takes up arms against God by ignoring him, and sin warrants God's judgment. To enjoy the pleasures of the flesh over the pleasures of God is "a sin of astonishing guilt, and not less odious to God, and damning in its nature."[13]

To lust after godless orgasms of the heart is death (Rom. 8:6). We are willing and guilty. We can find only one remedy to this comprehensive depravity, but we cannot find it inside of ourselves.

## Now What?

This is where act one in The Joy Project ends and the curtain closes. Total depravity is desperate helpless-

---

13   Ibid., 221.

ness. Each of us must get our life in order—but we are powerless to do it.

This is the essential self-awareness we need. "The doctrine of original sin is rude. It is the most incomprehensible of all the doctrines," said Tim Keller. "And yet without it, we become incomprehensible to ourselves."[14]

We must understand ourselves before we can comprehend God's Joy Project. And if self-awareness is essential, self-hate is powerless to remedy the problems we find in our hearts. Our eyes need to be pointed beyond ourselves altogether. "The Lord doesn't talk about your sin so you'll think you're trash," writes another modern-day Calvinist. "He talks about it just because you're not. He talks about it because he made you in his own image, with an infinitely higher and brighter plan for you than the one you chose for yourself."[15]

This is the plot twist. God points us *to* ourselves so that he might point us *away* from ourselves. He reveals our depravity so that we might consider his totality: the totality of his love, his goodness, and his beauty. He directs us *in* that he might direct us *out*— out toward his soul-satisfying joy.

It's clear, then, that in light of this human tragedy called "total depravity," our true and lasting joy depends on some bold and divine infringement on our self-destruction. If we are to live, someone must

---

14   Tim Keller, sermon, "Coming to Christ, Part 1" (February 4, 1990).
15   D. Clair Davis, "Personal Salvation," in *The Practical Calvinist: An Introduction to the Presbyterian and Reformed Heritage: In Honor of Dr. D. Clair Davis on the Occasion of His Seventieth Birthday*, ed. Peter A. Lillback (Fearn, Ross-shire: Christian Focus, 2002), 28.

intervene. Someone must break us. Someone must "batter our heart" and capture its worshiping gaze. We must be ravished, set free from our idols by a force of overwhelming and magnificent and superlative beauty. We don't need a list of practical solutions to get our lives in order; we need a loving God to invade our chaos.

Act 2:

# The Joy Project Designed

L eft to ourselves, we are stuck in our total depravity. The centripetal force of our affections keeps us gazing at ourselves. We turn away from God for our joy, and turn toward all we have left: money, sex, power, personal affirmation, Facebook friends, Twitter followers, and Instagram "likes." We use these old technologies (and we will use new technologies in the future) to tabulate our approval and then to use those metrics of approval to compare our popularity with others. When we do, we trade authentic glory for residual sludge. It's like drinking mud. And we choke.

To change the metaphor, we are a turbulent ocean, spinning hurricanes of hostility into the world. Our collective depravity spawns monsters: lies, bitter envy, heated controversy, wicked acts of terror, and world wars. We become those monsters, then paste on fake smiles. We are broken people, dysfunctional, focused on the petty, lured by empty idols, and driven by the mirage of human praise and popularity—we are simply sinners who need a great God to break into our lives.

And this is the big question: Will God stand back and permit all this depravity to manifest in the world with greater and more abundant destruction? Or will he simply wash creation with a flood, flush man down a cosmic sewer, and be done with it all? Will he fix this mess? Certainly he has the power to intervene, but does he want to? Will he rend the heavens and come down and step in to stop the downfall of twisted creatures bent on violence and self-destruction?

To find the answer, we hit pause on the earthly drama to look up into heaven and back into eternity past. This dark depravity in man's heart did not catch God by surprise. Before giving Adam the command not to eat from the one tree, God knew what would transpire. It was tragic and terrible, and yet remarkably man's fall into sin did not fall outside the scope of The Joy Project.

## Glimpses of God's Heart in Hosea

Hosea is a stunning book, filled to the brim with all the common depravities churning in the heart of man—lust, rebellion, idolatry. They're all there. Yet this tiny Old Testament book is not merely a tool for diagnosing the heart; it's also a story about relationship—about a husband (Hosea) and his marriage to a sexually promiscuous woman (Gomer).

The book of Hosea is shocking. The harlot becomes a wife and wanders away from her husband and reverts to her idolatrous pleasures. As readers, we desperately want her to return to her husband, but she refuses. She continues with her adulteries and lewd indulgences. What could slice more deeply into the heart of a husband? How should Hosea respond? Should he reject her and move on with his life? He doesn't. Hosea searches out his wife, redeems her, buys her freedom, and brings her back as his beloved wife.

This tale of idolatry and adultery is not a prime-time television drama, but a metaphor for God's incredible love for his wayward people, Israel. God's electing love for sinners resembles a dysfunctional marriage. Israel's sin grieves God. And yet it was tragically predictable for wayward hearts. Depraved sinners are nearly automatic in their rejection of God—they will choose to hide in religion and idolatry before ever turning to God for joy.

The pages of Hosea are drenched in sin's terror and despair. But as with many other tragic stories, it is ultimately a story of love, grace, and redemption. In the tragedy, we discover a doctrine cherished by the writers of the New Testament. In the pages of Hosea, amidst all this heartbreak, we find God's salvation wrapped up in the language of divine sovereignty and election. The God of Hosea is an electing God. He chooses. He initiates. He pursues. He saves from sins that self-destroy. Hosea is a book about marriage *because* it's a book about the God of election seeking out his blind bride.[1]

## Unconditional Election

This sovereign desire of God, from eternity past, to redeem sinners for himself is what is called "uncon-

---

1   See Hos. 9:10; 11:1; 13:5.

ditional election," the U in TULIP. From out of all the
God-ignoring sinners on earth, God will choose a
people for himself (a new bride). God will begin with
a whore and make himself a splendidly beautiful
bride. This bride is the object of his eternal love. She
will be pulled from the brothel of sin. It's all "unconditional," because like in the story of Hosea, it is not
based on any positive condition in Gomer's life. He
cannot love this new bride for her beauty; only his
unrelenting love will forge beauty in her.

Such language holds true across the Bible. God
makes this promise to sinners: "I will heal their
apostasy; I will love them freely, for my anger has
turned from them" (Hos. 14:4). This is the heart
behind God's electing love. God tenderly lures for
himself a wife, in time, by his unrelenting sovereign
grace (Hos. 2:14–23).

In the Old Testament, God's electing is seen most
clearly in his calling of a physical nation (Israel),
whereas in the New Testament, election is shown
from a spiritual standpoint. As we will see, the two
are deeply connected. In Hosea, we see that God
always planned to include not just the physical nation of Israel but also individuals from among the
Gentile pagan nations (Hos. 1:1–2:23). To prove this
point, the apostle Paul cites Hosea in Romans 9:22–
26. God's elect will be made into a bride from all the
world's people groups.

From among every race, God chooses men, wom-
en, children, ranchers, sailors, bankers, graphic de-
signers, the disabled, poets, schoolteachers, mer-
chants, athletes, and housewives. He even chooses

murderers, prostitutes, blindly religious people, and tax collectors. He chooses the soft-spoken and the brash. He chooses some who are famous, some who are geniuses, and some who are wealthy. But mostly he chooses nobodies (1 Cor. 1:18–31).

God does not elect every sinner. He chooses only some. Why? The apostle Paul addresses this hard and sobering question in Romans 9:22–23, where we're told that God's choice is his indisputable prerogative. His election is deeply personal. God will set his unstoppable love on sin-blind sinners, and this was his plan from eternity past. Depraved souls stuck in the unceasing cycle of sin and death will be the object of his love (Eph. 1:3–23), a reality that speaks not to the merit of the sinner but to the magnificence of God's love. And he loves to have it this way.

## Delighting to Love

God's love makes no accidents. The theme of God's electing love adorns the storyline of the Old Testament in other beautiful places, like this one: "Behold, to the LORD your God belong heaven and the heaven of heavens, the earth with all that is in it. Yet the LORD set his heart in love on your fathers and chose their offspring after them, you above all peoples, as you are this day" (Deut. 10:14–15).

God's election in Scripture is predicated on this foundational phrase: he "set his heart in love" on his chosen people (Deut. 7:7; 10:15). God's language for election is vivid and strong, writes John Piper: "The

LORD *delighted* in your fathers to love them."[2] To be elected is to be the object of God's delighting love.[3]

God delights to love us with the intensity that most of us can only perceive in the picture of romantic attraction and marriage. This love is not solemn or stifling. God's love for us is untamed and consuming.

The Old Testament has a lot to teach us about God's love. God's love is selective and exclusive. God's love is voluntary. God's love pursues—he seeks those with whom he desires a relationship of mutual delight. And God's love is self-originating: "It is not caused by any worth or attractiveness in its object, but rather creates worth in its object."[4]

## Pure Act of Pleasure (for Glory)

We see, then, that election is not merely the act of a pardoning judge who is disconnected, distant, and reluctant. God really has drawn close to us *because he wants to*. God delights to elect.

A passage that communicates the essence of God's heart in election is found in the new covenant prophecy of Jeremiah 32:41: "I will rejoice in doing them good, and I will plant them in this land in faithfulness, with all my heart and all my soul." It means

---

2   John Piper, *The Pleasures of God: Meditations on God's Delight in Being God* (Eugene, OR: Multnomah, 2000), 128–29n7.

3   For a sampling see Rom. 9:25; Col. 3:12; 1 Thess. 1:4–5; 2 Thess. 2:13.

4   My paragraph is a synopsis of the entry on בָּהֵב (love) in Willem VanGemeren, ed., *New International Dictionary of Old Testament Theology and Exegesis* (Grand Rapids, MI: Zondervan, 1997), 280–81.

God chooses people not simply out of pity, but out of delight.

In the history of the church, few theologians have grasped this reality more deeply—or have been more deeply grasped by it—than Puritan Thomas Goodwin. The seventeenth-century theologian defines election as God's "pure act of good pleasure." And he encourages Christians to "consider that God, in choosing you, not only loved you, but *delighted* to love you. It was not barely an act of will that he would choose some, he cared not whom, as being indifferent about it; but it was an act of love, and not of love only, but of good pleasure and of delight too. . . . God rejoiced over you from everlasting, in his intentions to do you good, with his whole heart and his whole soul."[5]

God loves because he takes infinite pleasure in his handiwork, his beloved people. Election displays God's whole heart and soul in action. God loves us with his entire heart and soul because our redemption from sin praises his infinite majesty. Goodwin wrestles with how to say this best, and eventually expresses it like this: "Look one way, and you think he loved us as if he regarded nothing else; look on the other side, and the glory of his grace does so appear that we seem to be forgotten, and God's glory alone shines in it."[6]

We are certainly not forgotten; these two angles are two angles on one glorious diamond. Angle one:

---

5  Thomas Goodwin, *The Works of Thomas Goodwin* (Edinburgh: James Nichol, 1863), 7:248. See also 9:424.
6  Goodwin, *Works*, 6:175.

God acts because the elect are on center stage and he is selflessly devoted to creating a church without spot or wrinkle. Angle two: God acts to take center stage to show himself the Supreme Being in the universe (1 Pet. 2:9). And it's both! Goodwin has tapped a profoundly glorious truth. In election, God pursues his own exaltation by inviting sinners to enjoy him forever. Hold this thought for now (it will develop later in the story).

For now, we can gather three principles concerning unconditional election:

- Election magnifies God's sovereign grace.
- Election highlights God's initiative to delight in a people.
- Election foreshadows God's desire to woo and win the hearts of sinners to enjoy his joy.

At that point in redemptive history, in eternity past, God placed on his elect an inestimable value, giving them worth beyond all treasures in the universe. Although they became frightfully twisted in their sin, God's chosen people have always been precious to him.[7]

But we are getting ahead of ourselves.

---

7    "When God hath chosen us, he takes delight in and is infinitely well pleased, both with this design and contrivement he hath towards us, and with our persons also, as considered in and through his beloved Son; even as a father that means to bestow his son upon such a woman, first takes a liking to the woman, (here is the love of goodwill,) which makes him choose her for his daughter, and pitch upon her, rather than upon any other, to make her his son's wife. But yet, when he hath betrothed her to his son, then he loves her with another and a further kind of love—he accepts her, he delights in her, and hath a complacency in her, as considering her to be his daughter, as wife unto this his son" (Goodwin, *Works* 1:109).

## Images of Grace

So how do we picture the reality of unconditional election?

Let me start with a personal example. My nine-year-old daughter dreamed of owning a hamster for years. She saved money, researched breeds, and read books about how to care for hamsters. Finally, she entered the local pet store with a purse full of cash, a head full of expertise, and a heart full of expectation.

"So what are you looking for in the perfect hamster?" I asked just before she left for the store. She shrugged her shoulders and admitted no conceived plans of what color she wanted. Her options were wide open (a smart strategy for a little girl wanting to ensure a hamster purchase). And so with an open mind and an open purse, she entered the pet store, found the three options, held each of them, evaluated fur colors, gauged personality types, and finally settled on a red haired male we now call Bilbo.

Bilbo is a specially chosen hamster who lives in a cage (and sleeps in a round tube). He is part of our family now. And while his story is a kind of election—it's not election in the biblical sense. Bilbo was elected because Bilbo was in stock. The election of God's Joy Project goes much, much deeper.

The beautiful marriage metaphor fits best. Unconditional election is the very first step toward a wedding, planned in eternity past. It sits so far back in time that no sinner on earth could see it coming. It is the first sight of a woman by a man, unbeknownst to her, from across a crowded room—a sight that will

lead to a conversation, which will lead to a relationship, which will lead to marriage vows. God's plan is
personal, but even older. He sets the wedding plans
in motion when he knows the name of the bride, but
the bride doesn't yet exist!

To make the marriage metaphor work, we must
stress one more clear distinction. The marriage of
election did not begin with the attractive beauty of
the bride. God made his redemptive move toward
his bride while she was morally unattractive. This
is pictured in the marriage of Hosea and Gomer: To
be elected by God is to be a specially chosen whore
pulled from a red-light brothel of idolatry.[8] We cannot make sense of election's beauty without its dark
backstory. In eternity past, God made up his mind.
He elected for himself depraved spiritual adulterers,
and he will love them for all eternity.[9]

So God's electing pursuit of us is settled and resolved. He alone initiates this love. His grace is unconditional and self-determined. There is nothing in
the elect—no beauty, no value, nothing within them
to attract God's love. What sinners receive from God
for their happiness is entirely unmerited. The worth
of God's elect is generated entirely by God's delight
in setting his love on them.[10]

We are invited to back up in time and to see
that before the creation of the universe God's heart
swelled with eager delight to redeem his people. To

8   Mark Seifrid, on Romans in the *Commentary on the New Testament Use of the Old Testament*, ed.
G. K. Beale and D. A. Carson (Grand Rapids, MI: Baker Academic, 2007), 647.
9   See Eph. 5:22–33.
10   D. A. Carson, *The Difficult Doctrine of the Love of God* (Wheaton, IL: Crossway, 2000), 18.

be predestined means God decreed your eternal joy prior to any foresight of faith or good works in you.[11] Knowing the depth of our total depravity, this truth should leave us totally staggered, in awe of his love, and eager to magnify him.

But here's the catch. God did not yet express his full delight in his elect before they were created. And he certainly could not express his full delight after the fall and entrance of sin into the world. God's delight in the elect remained unfulfilled at the point of predestination.[12] At this point in eternity past, the wedding day of full delight was still far off. But there will be a wedding. There will be an overflow of joy to come.

And this wedding plan led to an idea, a strategy, hatched between God the Father and God the Son. As Puritan John Flavel explains,

> In eternity past, the business transacted between them was the redemption and recovery of all God's elect. Our eternal happiness lay now before them, our dearest and everlasting concerns were now in their hands. The elect (though not yet in being) are here considered as existent, yes, and as fallen, miserable, forlorn creatures. How may these again be restored to happiness without

---

11 Jonathan Edwards, The "Miscellanies": (Entry Nos. 501–832), ed. Ava Chamberlain and Harry S. Stout, vol. 18, The Works of Jonathan Edwards (New Haven; London: Yale University Press, 2000), 282–83.

12 On this threefold delight over his children—election (amor benevolentiae), redemption (amor beneficentiae), and obedience (amor complacentiae vel amicitiae)—see Richard A. Muller, Post-Reformation Reformed Dogmatics (Grand Rapids, MI: Baker Academic, 2003), 3:561–9; and Francis Turretin, Institutes of Elenctic Theology (Phillipsburg, NJ: P&R, 1992), 1:242.

*prejudice to the honor, justice and truth of God?
This, this is the business that lay before them.*[13]

Yes, redemption is the great business of God's Joy
Project, and it will require further action on God's
part to preserve his holiness and to provide us true
joy.

## Action Required

This much is clear at this point: God's depraved elect
need more than promises and plans—they need
God to *do something*. God may woo with words, but
he will only draw his bride through deeds. For a holy
God to find his full delight in his sinful children,
and for them to delight in him, he must initiate redemptive action. This is how it has always worked.
Electing love erupts into the world through feats of
redemption, such as a rescue from Egypt in the first
Exodus (Deut. 4:37; 7:8).

The eternal delight of God must confront the real
darkness of human depravity. His Joy Project hinges
on a new redemptive act.

When the time was just right, a special elect Son
would arrive, a Son led by the Spirit and cherished
by his Father above all else. This Son would arrive
as a mighty deliverer, a Son who would walk out of
Egypt's sand and step through the waters. He would

---

13   John Flavel, *The Whole Works of the Reverend John Flavel* (London: W. Baynes & Son, 1820),
1:54–55.

mark the dawn of a new work of God—a second deliverance. A new exodus.[14]

---

14  A summary of Hos. 11:1; Isa. 42:1; and Matt. 3:16–17.

Act 3:

# The Joy Project Purchased

God's elaborate plan to redeem a people for himself hinges on a second exodus. It would echo the first Exodus, but be fundamentally different. It would require an anointed Son to walk out of Egypt and through the waters—a Son in whom God would express his great delight. In this Son, God's eternal plan of election would be manifested in space, time, blood, and water.

The entire Joy Project waited on Jesus, God's own Son, God's beloved, the anointed, the chosen one. Christ fits into this huge unfolding plan of election as the specially chosen (or elected) Son.

## The Story of Election

I have mentioned election several times already, but because it occupies a major place in God's plan, we need a brief sketch and summary of this concept. In the sweeping storyline of the Bible, election was first applied to God's choice of Israel from all other nations. Later, election focused specifically on King David, God's chosen king. Then God promised that he would send his people an even better servant, a king to be born in the city of David. This promise was fulfilled in the Christmas birth of Jesus Christ. Soon after, election was realized in the calling and faith of the disciples closest to Jesus. Eventually in the Bible, election will find its fullest expression in the gathering of the believing Jews and Gentiles brought together in the church.

As this story of election unfolds, Christ is the centerpiece. Christ is the epicenter of election, the Ground Zero of God's Joy Project. However you put it, the story of election reaches a pinnacle in divine words that split the sky: "This is my Son, my Chosen One; listen to him!" (Luke 9:35). Or again at the baptism of Jesus: "This is my beloved Son, with whom I am well pleased" (Matt. 3:17). When God calls to himself his chosen children, it includes only those who are found *in the elected Son* (Eph. 1:3–14). In Christianity, the concept of election is foremost a reference to Christ. God elects, chooses, and sets before himself an object of infinite delight. This is Christ.

To a superior degree, God's beloved Son proves that electing grace and eternal joy cannot be separated. The aim of God's electing grace is eternal joy.[1]

## The Plan in Review

At this point, we must be reminded again of the chaos of fallen creation (T—total depravity) and God's intent to redeem it (U—unconditional election). This entire plan of redemption hinges on the life and work of Christ (L—limited atonement). Limited atonement—or better, *definite atonement*—helps

---

1   See Rom. 9:25; Col 3:12; 1 Thess. 1:4–5; 2 Thess. 2:13.

to explain why Jesus put such a strong emphasis on election.[2]

As the middle letter of TULIP, (L) *limited atonement* is a way of explaining that Jesus, by his death and resurrection, purchased redemption for the elect. In the words of Piper, the L means "indestructible joy in God is infallibly secured for us by the blood of the covenant." "Infallibly secured" is a good way to say it, because in this unbreakable joy-security we discover God's infallible aim to redeem lost sinners.

## The Joy of Jesus

Despite being the "Man of Sorrows," Jesus displayed his happiness, too. The most joy-filled outburst recorded from the life of Christ is found in Luke 10, where Jesus sent out seventy-two of his followers to preach and heal, to serve sinners in word and deed. As they hustled off in every direction to all the neighboring villages, Jesus turns to lament the unbelief of so many sinners who refused to trust in him.

In stark contrast to unbelief, the seventy-two disciples went out and saw magnificent spectacles unfold before their eyes, as they wielded the power of Christ over demons. They soon returned to Jesus, breathless, amazed by their power over evil. But Jesus was careful to redirect their enthusiasm to higher realities: "Nevertheless, do not rejoice in this, that the spirits are subject to you, but rejoice that your names are written in heaven" (Luke 10:20).

---

2   Jesus explains election in places such as John 6:35–45; 17:1–10, 24–26.

Minutes later, with a heart overflowing with gratitude, Jesus demonstrated the God-wardness of his ecstatic trinitarian pleasure:

> In that same hour he rejoiced in the Holy Spirit and said, "I thank you, Father, Lord of heaven and earth, that you have hidden these things from the wise and understanding and revealed them to little children; yes, Father, for such was your gracious will. All things have been handed over to me by my Father, and no one knows who the Son is except the Father, or who the Father is except the Son and anyone to whom the Son chooses to reveal him." (Luke 10:21–22)

Puritan David Clarkson sums up the story well:

> We find Christ in an ecstasy, almost transported with joy. His spirit leaped within him, and as though he had been rapt into heaven, adds praises, his joy breaks forth into thanks. But what is the occasion of both? Not that the devils were subject through his name, but that it pleased the Father to make known the mysteries of salvation to despised men. Christ seemed to make man, of all earthly things, his chief joy on earth; this revived him, joyed his heart in the midst of his sorrows and sufferings—that man should be thereby made happy.[3]

3  David Clarkson, *The Works of David Clarkson* (Edinburgh, 1864), 3:34.

God's sovereign plan to redeem sinners and to fill them with joy fills Jesus with vigorous joy. This intertwined tapestry of joy-sharing was all designed by God in The Joy Project, and this is why nowhere else in the Gospels do we see Jesus overjoyed like this. The joy of Jesus is the joy of unconditional election. The blinding power of sin is broken and the eyes of sinners are opened to the all-satisfying vision of God's glory. Election is the project, the project works, and Jesus is thrilled!

Luke 10 offers us a unique glimpse into how Christ prized election and how it fueled his joy. But the harsh reality is that the entire plan of election hinged on the atoning death of the Chosen One. Jesus knew that for God's Joy Project to materialize in full, he had to shed his blood. Shed blood secured sovereign joy. More on that in a moment.

But what about those who refuse to come to Christ? Before we leave Luke 10, note how the joy-giving grace of election is never used to excuse unbelief of God-ignoring sinners. In this same chapter, Christ both rejoiced in the faith of elect sinners headed to eternal life (Luke 10:21–22) and wept over the rebellious unbelief of sinners. Those who are blind to the glory of Christ, and unwilling to repent and run to him, remain under God's wrath and face eternal destruction for their sins (Luke 10:13–16).

## Blood for Joy

Given what's at stake eternally, Luke 10 is our front-row seat to see how much Christ prized the plan of election and how it fueled his joy with his Father. But we have not detailed *definite atonement*, the heart of God's plan of election.

The entire Joy Project hinges on the person and work of Christ, as Jonathan Edwards so vividly explains. Christ created the world (Col. 1:16). But even more amazing, he lived (and died) *inside* this creation. Don't miss this. "For the creator to make the creature was a great thing; but for him to become a creature was a greater thing. And he did a much greater thing still to obtain joy; in that for this he laid down his life, and suffered even the death of the cross: for this he poured out his soul unto death, and he that is the Lord of the universe, God over all, blessed for evermore, offered himself a sacrifice, in both body and soul, in the flames of divine wrath. Christ obtains his elect spouse by conquest."

Christ entered the world on a joy conquest. He must conquer and overcome every obstacle and enemy that stands in the way of The Joy Project. Therefore, Christ "encountered these enemies in the greatest battle that ever was beheld by men or angels: he fought with principalities and powers; he fought alone with the powers of darkness, and all the armies of hell; yea, he conflicted with the infinitely more dreadful wrath of God, and overcame in this great battle; and thus he obtained his spouse."[4]

---

4  Jonathan Edwards, "The Church's Marriage to Her Sons, and to Her God," in *Sermons and Discourses, 1743–1758*, ed. Wilson H. Kimnach and Harry S. Stout, vol. 25, *The Works of Jonathan Edwards* (New Haven, CT: Yale University Press, 2006), 187–88.

## Limited Atonement

God's Joy Project is part cosmic battle. And when the dust settles from the conquering victory of Christ's life, death, and resurrection, we discover seven key connections between his work and God's Joy Project.

1. *Christ's death proved sufficient.* When Roman soldiers drove spikes into the wrists of Christ and lifted him up in the air, he died a death that was sufficient to pay for every sin of the entire world, sufficient to save everyone on planet earth. Nothing lacked in Christ's death or resurrection. In this sense, it was infinite atonement.

Despite the belief of universalists (who hold the unbiblical idea that every person will eventually be saved), the all-sufficient atonement of Christ is applied only to some, to the elect—to those who truly come to faith. Christ's atonement was so powerful, that not a drop of human effort adds anything to the redemption-accomplishing blood of Christ.[5] Human repentance and faith are essential to the plan, as we will see later, but salvation is not grounded on the enterprise of man. Salvation is grounded in the initiative of Christ and his death.

2. *Christ's death secured salvation.* The cross did not merely make salvation possible. The cross is not like a single who secures a wedding date and reserves an elegant church years before finding a mate, hoping they will find someone in the meantime. No, Christ's death secured salvation for the elect individually, *by name.* In his death, Christ effectually pursues a bride

---

5  Titus 3:5–6 is a prime example.

by entering the brothel of idolatry to grab hold of the elect, one by one, by name, and pulling them out from the bondage of sin. In this way Christ *achieved* redemption at the cross, a point John Piper explains well:

> *If we want to go deeper in our experience of God's grace, this is an ocean of love for us to enjoy. God does not mean for the bride of his Son to only feel loved with general, world-embracing love. He means for her to feel ravished with the specificity of his affection that he set on her before the world existed. He means for us to feel a focused: "I chose you. And I send my Son to die to have you." This is what we offer the world. We don't horde it for ourselves. And we don't abandon it by saying, all we have to offer the world is God's general love for all people. No, we offer this. We offer a full and complete and definite atonement. We offer Christ. We don't say, come to a possibility. We say, come to Christ. Receive Christ. And what we promise them if they come is that they will be united to him and his bride. And all that he bought for his bride will be theirs. All that he secured with absolute certainty will be their portion forever.*[6]

---

6   John Piper, *Five Points: Towards a Deeper Experience of God's Grace* (Fearn, Ross-shire: Christian Focus, 2013), 52.

God designed it to unfold in this way. Christ will die, God will justify the elect, and the justified will be filled with joy in Jesus.[7]

3. *Christ purchased faith.* Christ died not to ensure that salvation *can happen*, but to ensure that salvation *will happen*. At the cross, Christ purchased every grace the elect need for justification, sanctification, and glorification. At the cross, Christ even purchased the act of personal faith, a gift the elect will use later in the story.[8]

4. *The cross sets a pattern for Christ's ongoing work.* His earthly ministry, death on the cross, and resurrection show a deep love and concern for the elect. His concern continues today. In his ongoing high priestly ministry, the focus of Christ is on the elect. Right now, as our interceding High Priest, Christ prays not for the entire world. He prays specifically for the spiritual flourishing of the elect (John 17:9).

5. *Christ's definite atonement was motivated by joy.* Imagine it. If Jesus burst out in ecstatic thanks for the blessing of a few elect disciples, how deep and rich must have been the manifold joy driving him to achieve in the cross the faith and full atonement for all the elect in the history of the church (Heb. 12:2)?

6. *Christ's blood defeated every impediment to joy.* In the blood of Christ, every obstacle to the happiness of his people was defeated—sin, selfishness, Satan, death, condemnation. Every enemy of ultimate and eternal joy was defeated, broken, and paid for.

---

7 See Rom. 5:2–3, 5; 8:33.
8 See Eph. 2:7–8; Phil. 1:29.

Christ's death paved the way for the elect to find unhindered eternal pleasures in the presence of God.

7. *Christ's blood purchased the joy of the new covenant.* God's promise to break into human depravity to redeem the world did not (and cannot) rest on the initiative of sinners (Ezek. 11:19; 36:26). Instead, his promise rests on the blood of Christ. His blood inaugurated a new covenant of grace and it secured for the elect an entrance into the joys of God (Matt. 26:28).[9]

In the marvelous achievements of our Savior, we affirm bold statements like these: "Jesus Christ creates and confirms and purchases with his blood the new covenant and the everlasting joy of our relationship with God."[10] Or, "That's what Christ bought for us when he died and shed the blood of the new covenant. He bought for us the gift of joy in God."[11] What's more, the joy we have is God's own: "Christ purchased for us spiritual joy and comfort, which is in a participation of God's joy and happiness."[12]

Christ died to pull us into the joy of God. How exactly does this happen in our lives? The answer brings us one step closer to fully understanding God's Joy Project.

9  See the joy of Jer. 31:12–14 in the new covenant context of Jer. 31:31–40; also Joel 3:18 and Heb. 12:22–24.

10  John Piper and Justin Taylor, eds., *Sex and the Supremacy of Christ* (Wheaton, IL: Crossway, 2005), 29.

11  John Piper, *When I Don't Desire God: How to Fight for Joy* (Wheaton, IL: Crossway: 2013), 53.

12  Jonathan Edwards, *Writings on the Trinity, Grace, and Faith*, ed. Sang Hyun Lee and Harry S. Stout, vol. 21, *The Works of Jonathan Edwards* (New Haven, CT: Yale University Press, 2003), 136.

## Holy Spirit Joy

In John 17 we overhear another glorious prayer between Jesus and his Father. As we eavesdrop, we
hear the Son recount his motivation to glorify the
Father. To that end, God has given to the Son a bride
to be called out of the world and kept safe by him.
The Son's redemption of the bride will magnify the
Father. In this context, Jesus prays that his joy would
be shared by the elect souls the Father has given to
him. It's a glorious chapter, with God's plan for *election* and *joy* interlocking once again.

But it raises an important question: How exactly does the joy of Jesus find its way into the hearts
of the elect? Here's the short answer: by the work of
God the Holy Spirit. The Father sent his elect Son,
the Son shed his blood to purchase all the blessings
of redemption, and the Holy Spirit applies these
blood-bought blessings into the lives of God's elect.

After Jesus died and rose and ascended into
heaven, he poured out his Spirit upon all those who
believed his good news. This is the inspiring connection between the definite atonement of Christ
and the joy of the elect. Christ does not give the
life-transforming power of the Holy Spirit to everyone. The Spirit is the special, saving possession of
God's chosen.[13]

And where the Spirit of the Lord is, there is joy.[14]

Few theologians better grasped this Spirit-joy
connection than Jonathan Edwards. He wrote, "The

13  See Isa. 42:1; Gal. 4:6; 1 Thess. 1:4–5; 1 Pet. 1:1–2.
14  See Luke 10:21; Acts 13:52; Rom. 14:17; Gal. 5:22; 1 Thess. 1:6.

Holy Spirit is the great purchase of Christ."[15] "All the blessedness of the redeemed consists in their partaking of Christ's fullness, which consists in partaking of that Spirit which is given not by measure unto him."[16] "The Holy Spirit, in his indwelling, in his influences, and in his fruits, is the sum of all grace, holiness, comfort and joy. In one word, the Holy Spirit is the entire spiritual good that Christ purchased for men in this world. The Holy Spirit is also the sum of all perfection, glory, and eternal joy that he purchased for them in eternity."[17] All these glorious realities come to us through God the Holy Spirit. His role is decisive in filling our lives with the joy of Christ.

The implication of this is summarized well by Charles Spurgeon: "Think not that Christ has merely put joys within our reach that we may get for ourselves, but he comes and puts the joys inside our hearts."[18] This joy-of-Christ-put-in-me is the work of the Spirit.

## "L" and Joy

In all these ways (and others), joy springs from Christ's blood for the elect. In its concentrated form, here's what Christ's joy looks like:

15  Jonathan Edwards, *Ethical Writings,* ed. Paul Ramsey and John E. Smith, vol. 8, *The Works of Jonathan Edwards* (New Haven; London: Yale University Press, 1989), 353.

16  Edwards, *Writings on the Trinity,* 136.

17  Jonathan Edwards, *Apocalyptic Writings: "Notes on the Apocalypse" An Humble Attempt,* ed. John E. Smith and Stephen J. Stein, vol. 5, *The Works of Jonathan Edwards* (New Haven, CT: Yale University Press, 1977), 341.

18  C. H. Spurgeon, *The Metropolitan Tabernacle Pulpit Sermons,* vol. 11 (London: Passmore & Alabaster, 1865), 633.

- Jesus found exuberant delight in the Father's plan to save the elect.
- Jesus desired that his joy in the Father, through the Spirit, would overflow in the lives of God's children.
- Jesus died to redeem the elect, to become their High Priest, and to guarantee their eternal flourishing.
- Jesus's blood defeated every ultimate impediment to the joy of God's chosen.
- Jesus's blood purchased for the elect the promised joys of the new covenant.
- Jesus's blood purchased the Holy Spirit, opening an eternal fountain of eternal joy in the life of the elect, which is the joy of Christ in them.

Understanding the depths of these concentrated truths will take an eternity of study, reflection, and worship.

## Out of the Water

Can we find greater or more glorious news? Jesus entered the world on a mission to shed his blood and rise from the dead in order to secure our joy forever! So breathe deep. True, unending joy is not the result of the right storage gimmicks, organizational hacks, or healthy habits.

The entire focus of The Joy Project centers on the broad, heaving shoulders of Christ on a God-forsaken cross. All the glorious themes in this plan converge in the ancient prophecy of Isaiah 42:1:

*Behold my servant, whom I uphold,*
    *my chosen, in whom my soul delights;*
*I have put my Spirit upon him,*
    *he will bring forth justice to the nations.*

These four lines capture the truly awesome drama played out in Christ, beginning in his baptism, where "the Holy Spirit descended on him in bodily form, like a dove; and a voice came from heaven, 'You are my beloved Son; with you I am well pleased'" (Luke 3:22). The elect Son emerged from the waters of baptism, the Father spoke his delight from heaven, and the Holy Spirit descended into human history. The stage was set for the story to take a new turn, a turn that gets personal, deeply particular, and irresistibly individual.

Act 4:

# The Joy Project Breaks and Enters

W e now pick up where act one ended, in the unfolding drama of life on this fallen planet.

Pull back the curtains on the powers at work in this world, and you will discover two of the strongest forces on earth: pride and despair. One generates what seems to be tremendous dedication and focus; the other sucks all motivation and concentration from life. In the clutches of pride or despair, much of mankind gets stuck—trapped by self-glory or pinned down by hopelessness. Both alienate us; both dull us to true joy.

Few possess the perception to see so clearly behind this curtain and to explain what they see with more bone-chilling reality than David Foster Wallace. In his novel *Infinite Jest* he exposes the human love affair with entertainment, the high-octane drive for personal glory, the prison of drug addiction, and the nightmarish isolation of depression. For a thousand pages, through a cast of characters, he exposes the world's dark plagues of pride and despair.

## The Pride Trap

Wallace introduces us to LaMont Chu, an eleven-year-old athletic prodigy with "an increasingly crippling obsession with tennis fame." He desperately wants his picture in glossy magazines. He yearns for television commentators in jackets and headsets to celebrate his every move on the court. He wants endorsements. He lusts for hype. He longs for the worship of photographers. LaMont's greatest threats in life are the inevitable losses on the court and the unavoidable injuries to his body.

"Why," his friend Lyle asks, "are you driven to this fame?"

"I guess to give my life some sort of kind of meaning," he answers honestly.

LaMont burns for something to give his life meaning and substance. But like a good friend, Lyle tries to talk real sense into LaMont by explaining how fame decomposes the heart. "The first photograph, the first magazine, the gratified surge, the seeing themselves as others see them, the hagiography of image, perhaps. Perhaps this first time: *enjoyment*. After that . . . they do not feel what you burn for. . . . Something changes. After the first photograph has been in a magazine, the famous men do not *enjoy* their photographs in magazines so much as they fear that their photographs will cease to appear in magazines. They are trapped, just as you are."[1]

The lust for fame and the need to preserve fame are twin traps that cannot sustain life's meaning or

---

1   David Foster Wallace, *Infinite Jest* (New York: Little, Brown, 1996), 388–89.

the soul's pleasure. Craving for self-glory is to hunger for food that does not exist; it is to feed a fire that cannot die by feeding it. It is to be suffocated by constant fears and growing isolation.

## The Despair Snare

Despair finds a similar destination, but across a different route. Throughout the novel, David Foster Wallace walks the reader through the various layers of depression in a Dante-like descent.

He begins with *anhedonia*, a simple melancholy. At this level, "the devoted wife and mother finds the thought of her family about as moving, all of a sudden, as a theorem of Euclid." Anhedonia is life hollowed of joys, a shell of dull detachment. Such a woman can still recall memories of happiness, and she may even talk about happiness, but only in principle. She *feels* none of it. The melancholy anhedonic becomes "Unable to Identify." Uprooted and lost, she is emotionally disconnected from the world and her home, floating through life in a daze, anesthetized, and abstracted from reality.

This type of depression is reserved especially for the characters in Wallace's book who center their lives on professional goals. In mid-life, they discover the joys they have expected through all their strivings have evaporated. Winded from the blow of this revelation, they realize that all along they've merely been chasing the carrot of superiority and money, and the only prize, all that's left to them, is numb emptiness. Anhedonia.

But this stage of melancholy is a vacation compared to "the Great White Shark of pain," a "predator-grade depression," an anguish and despair so dark it simply goes by the name *It*:

> *It is a level of psychic pain wholly incompatible with human life as we know it. . . . It is lonely on a level that cannot be conveyed. . . . If a person in physical pain has a hard time attending to anything except that pain, a clinically depressed person cannot even perceive any other person or thing as independent of the universal pain that is digesting her, cell by cell. Everything is part of the problem, and nothing is the solution. It is a hell for one.*[2]

If you've come close to this killer, or know someone who has, you know there's no simple cure for clinical depression (and Christians are certainly not immune from serious depression[3]). But the characters in Wallace's novel pursue just about any medical option to escape the pain, even temporarily. Those tormented by the relentless *It* simply want to be numb again, to return to a place where they feel no pain or pleasure, a place to escape the ravishing pain and the dry rot they now feel eating away inside. They stand at the open window of a tall burning building, with flames

2  Ibid.
3  If you struggle with depression you're not alone. Along with reaching out to your doctor and your pastor, here are three excellent books to consider, all written by Calvinists who are familiar with depression: Ed Welch, *Depression: Looking Up from the Stubborn Darkness* (New Growth, 2011); John Piper, *When the Darkness Will Not Lift: Doing What We Can While We Wait for God—and Joy* (Crossway, 2007); and David Murray, *Christians Get Depressed Too* (Reformation Heritage, 2010).

roaring below, pressed for a decision: burn or jump? That is the daily decision of those living under the oppressive nightmare of *It*.[4]

## We Are What We Love

Pride and despair hollow out our very existence, because at the root of our identity, we know we are made to love. David Foster Wallace tells us what we already know (and what Lewis said to us earlier): "You are what you love."[5] We love, he says, because we are "absolutely dying to give ourselves away to something."[6] Pride and despair are traps that make this glorious end of giving ourselves to others truly impossible.

We must give ourselves away because we are made for transcendence. We are made to find an approval and a home that we cannot ever seem to find here. We are made for a temple. As another character in his novel suggests:

> *Someone taught that temples are for fanatics only and took away the temples and promised there was no need for temples. And now there is no shelter. And no map for finding the shelter of a temple. And you all stumble about in the dark, this confusion of permissions. This without-end pursuit of a happiness of which someone let you*

4    Ibid., 692–98.
5    Ibid., 107.
6    David Lipsky, *Although of Course You End Up Becoming Yourself: A Road Trip with David Foster Wallace* (New York: Broadway: 2010), 81.

*forget the old things which made happiness pos-sible.*[7]

Wallace is on to something profoundly important here. We cannot find our way to joy by looking inside. We are guided by no inner spiritual hunches, no inner spiritual light, no inner guiding pings that can lead us to a temple of spiritual shelter. We are made to worship, but we cannot find the right temple. We stumble along without a map, we grope in the dark, but we get stuck in our own repeating loops of despair.

Wallace once explained this point in a commencement address:

> *There is no such thing as not worshipping. Everybody worships. The only choice we get is what to worship. . . . If you worship money and things, if they are where you tap real meaning in life, then you will never have enough, never feel you have enough. It's the truth. Worship your body and beauty and sexual allure and you will always feel ugly. And when time and age start showing, you will die a million deaths before they finally grieve you. On one level, we all know this stuff already. It's been codified as myths, proverbs, clichés, epigrams, parables; the skeleton of every great story. The whole trick is keeping the truth up front in daily consciousness.*

7   Wallace, *Infinite Jest*, 319–20.

*Worship power, you will end up feeling weak and afraid, and you will need ever more power over others to numb you to your own fear. Worship your intellect, being seen as smart, you will end up feeling stupid, a fraud, always on the verge of being found out.*

*But the insidious thing about these forms of worship is not that they're evil or sinful, it's that they're unconscious. They are default settings. They're the kind of worship you just gradually slip into, day after day, getting more and more selective about what you see and how you measure value without ever being fully aware that that's what you're doing.*[8]

On the contrary, there *is* sin here—sin so strong and so deep we have no hope of escaping our false gods on our own.

Unable (and unwilling) to find our way to the temple of Joy, we worship appearance, sex, money, and intellect. In our pride, we worship the wrong things, which lead to despair, more pride, and more despair. In this cycle we are stuck. Our lives may not be as boldly self-centered as the tennis prodigy, and we may never get trapped inside the nightmare of *It*, but we all are familiar with cycles of pride and melancholy. We know what it's like to be enslaved by the vanity of praise or to be deadened by despair. We know what it's like to be lost in sadness and unable to find our way to the safe shelter of joy (Ps. 43:4).

---

8   David Foster Wallace, commencement address at Kenyon College, May 21, 2005.

This is what it means to be lost in the pain and confusion of a fallen world. Wallace's novel echoes with autobiographical tragedy, written by a remarkably perceptive author who desperately needed to find his way to the true temple but apparently never did (John 2:19).

David Foster Wallace hanged himself at the age of forty-six.

## Novocain for the Soul

Pride and despair work together like a needle of Novocain slipped into the soul. Without grace, we are numb to true spiritual sensation.

Compounding the problem, we can't perceive the thick darkness and the degree of our desperation. In a broken world of conflicting emotions, in the chaos of self-motivation, and in the depression that smothers and enslaves us, we cannot escape. We cannot escape ourselves. We aren't even aware that we need to escape, which is much worse. We are bound; we are immobilized; we are confined by the blinded self.

Even if we perceive all this, and identify the forces of pride and despair, and pinpoint their effects in our hearts, we remain hopeless. Our only chance of deliverance is hope—hope in God's sovereign grace to reach down and pull us from this world's dark despair. God's sovereign grace must find exiled sinners who pursue self-glory, who live in a "confusion of permissions," who obscure evil for good. Every one of us must be freed from the prison of self.

John Donne put this desperation to poetry four hundred years before David Foster Wallace. Donne wrote, prayed, and pleaded with God in his famous Holy Sonnet to be overthrown from his own temptations:

*Batter my heart, three-person'd God, for you*
     *As yet but knock, breathe, shine, and seek to mend;*
*That I may rise and stand, o'erthrow me, and bend*
     *Your force to break, blow, burn, and make me new.*
*I, like an usurp'd town to another due,*
     *Labor to admit you, but oh, to no end;*
*Reason, your viceroy in me, me should defend,*
     *But is captiv'd, and proves weak or untrue.*
*Yet dearly I love you, and would be lov'd fain,*
     *But am betroth'd unto your enemy;*
*Divorce me, untie or break that knot again,*
     *Take me to you, imprison me, for I,*
*Except you enthrall me, never shall be free,*
     *Nor ever chaste, except you ravish me.*

The affection-driven language in the sonnet is graphic. Whether or not he intended it, John Donne put irresistible grace to bold verse. It's a story that unfolds in three metaphors. First, we are broken sinners who need the triune God to reshape and recreate our heart's longings. Second, our hearts are like overrun towns governed by God's enemy, and we must have this evil dictator overthrown and run out.

Third, we are betrothed to our evil desires and pleasures. Again, we cannot escape. The last two lines are the most poignant. God must overcome us and awaken us to superior pleasures in him. Until God acts on us, we are lost.

## Ravished Free by Sovereign Grace

Donne's language is dangerously affectionate, but appropriately shocking if we are really as desperate as the Bible says. And we are. We must be remade for God. We must get new hearts from God. We must find our new identity in God. But we keep falling back on ourselves. We are broken. We are weak. We are distortions of what God intends. We can't control what we want. We can't control what we feel.

John Donne, and others before him, were startled by the darkness they saw in the world—and in their own souls. So they searched every page of Holy Scripture to find the strongest possible words to articulate the mystery of this overriding redemption. How could God reach into time and space and break through these imprisoning walls of smugness, cynicism, self-hate, and all those unutterable forces of self-destruction? What is God's battering ram to retake the city of our hearts?

To answer those questions, the Puritans in the seventeenth century turned to the romantically charged language of the Bible to illustrate God's wooing of his bride:

*I will allure her,*

*and bring her into the wilderness,*
*and speak tenderly to her. (Hos. 2:14)*

*I led them with cords of kindness,*
*with the bands of love. (Hos. 11:4)*

*Draw me after you; let us run. (Song 1:4)*

Those passages ring true for us. We know that God must lure us to himself, but we are deaf to his wooing words. First, he must break the siren song of pride and despair in our lives. And he does, as we see from the way in which redemptive history has progressed. During his time on earth, Jesus said:

*The hour is coming, and is now here, when the true worshipers will worship the Father in spirit and truth, for the Father is seeking such people to worship him. (John 4:23)*

*No one can come to me unless the Father who sent me draws him. And I will raise him up on the last day. (John 6:44)*

*No one can come to me unless it is granted him by the Father. (John 6:65)*

*My sheep hear my voice, and I know them, and they follow me. I give them eternal life, and they will never perish, and no one will snatch them out of my hand. My Father, who has given them to me, is greater than all. (John 10:27–29)*

> I, when I am lifted up from the earth, will draw
> all people [Jew and Gentile alike] to myself. (John
> 12:32)

God chooses his children, breaks their sin with blood, lures them out of the mire of pride and despair, and draws them to himself in order to love and delight in them.

> Those who were not my people I will call "my
> people," and her who was not beloved I will call
> "beloved." (Rom. 9:25)

> As God's chosen ones, holy and beloved . . . (Col.
> 3:12)

> For we know, brothers loved by God, that he has
> chosen you, because our gospel came to you not
> only in word, but also in power. (1 Thess. 1:4–5)

> We ought always to give thanks to God for you,
> brothers beloved by the Lord, because God chose
> you as the firstfruits to be saved, through sanc-
> tification by the Spirit and belief in the truth. (2
> Thess. 2:13)

The Father elects, searches out, and draws; the Son attracts and secures; all by the power of the Holy Spirit. In his death and resurrection, Christ acted on behalf of his beloved, not only to secure their redemption (definite atonement) but to draw them out of sin and into his delight.

## Breaking Bad

What all this means is that, even if we practiced the most devout religion on earth, we could not get inside the right temple. Apart from grace, our religious devotion alone works only to make proud people more arrogant or miserable people more dejected. Human religion can only feed the sinner's pride or fuel the sinner's despair.

"Only Christianity destroys both pride *and* despair," says Tim Keller. "Christianity first shows you a law that has to be totally fulfilled, destroying your pride. Then Christianity shows you a Savior who has totally fulfilled it, getting rid of your despair."[9] Christ saves us from our two major faults: "he ransomed us from our self-honoring reactions to success, and our self-hating responses to failure."[10]

In the pain, pride, and despair of this fallen world, helpless sinners desperately depend on God's wooing, alluring, tender, and unstoppably sovereign grace. God once extended it to me. And he extends it to you.

## Sovereign Joy

But what does all this drawing and alluring look like? In the words of Puritan Thomas Goodwin, God first puts "an instinct into the heart after Christ." The elect do not wake up one day and break free from all

---

9   Tim Keller, sermon, "Jesus, Our Priest" (November 12, 1995).
10   Tim Keller, *Judges for You, God's Word for You* (Epsom, Surrey, UK: Good Book Company; 2013), 99.

pride and despair with a heart full of love for Christ. No, it doesn't work like that.

We have a moment of immediate change, but we don't (unfortunately) shed all sin; rather, it is "by a still and secret touch of the heart . . . such as when the iron is touched with the loadstone."[11] A small piece of steel, when magnetized, will forever point north. So too the soul, when God has touched it, will orient toward Christ. This is the first evidence of the sovereign initiative of God acting on the soul, giving the soul a newborn instinct toward the beauty of Christ. This is called "regeneration."

Regeneration is a new instinct inside of us that draws us toward a superior beauty. Augustine called this a "victorious delight," powerful enough to trump every "carnal delight." We will see this work out in Augustine's life in a moment.

In other words, for God to pull off his Joy Project, new delights will go to war with old delights. Greater delights must conquer lesser delights. What Augustine called the "victorious delights" is the result of God's working—as gentle as a spring rain, as powerful as a resurrection, as gruesome as a battle.

### Violent Grace

Every sinner is offered two objects of supreme delight: the pleasures of the world or the pleasures of Christ. We all naturally take the pleasures of this world; we know no other way. The world offers us

---

11 Thomas Goodwin, *The Works of Thomas Goodwin* (Edinburgh, 1864), 8:573–75.

riches, glory, indulgence, ease, and comfort to the sinful flesh. Christ offers everlasting joy. He offers free, full, and final pardon for sins; peace and reconciliation with God; and pleasures forever in heaven.

The human heart must now be compelled toward a greater good. We need a new power and a victorious delight that will make Christ the most beautiful thing in the universe to us. So the Holy Spirit gets to work. Writes Puritan John Flavel:

> *The power of God does not act against the freedom of man's will, by co-action and force; no, but of unwilling he makes it willing; taking away the obstinacy and reluctance of the will by the efficacy of his grace, a sweet and pleasant victory. Beasts are driven and forced against their passions, but men drive and force themselves. When God seeks to bring home a poor sinner, he cannot resist the power of God's Spirit, that draws him. The soul comes freely by the consent of his will; for this is the method of Christ in drawing souls to him.*[12]

If our greatest problem—our *total depravity*—is our failure to treasure God, then our greatest need in life is to come alive to God's beauty. This is the work of *regeneration*. Regeneration is the infusion of God's life into my spiritual deadness so that I can now behold his resplendence.

---

12   John Flavel, *The Whole Works of the Reverend John Flavel* (London: W. Baynes & Son, 1820), 4:92–93.

It's exactly what we need for God's Joy Project to take root in us. In sin, our reason loses its way because its compass is not pointed toward God. In sin, our will and desires go off course because they have no captain at the helm. Grace fixes the compass and sets our course, putting our reason, will, and desires on a fixed course toward God and toward genuine joy.

Regeneration renovates our minds, snaps the power of our sin, and sets our souls running after Jesus. Free from the enslaving power of sin, we discover the grand secret to what it means to be genuinely and thoroughly Christian—the joy of Christ.[13]

## Regeneration and Faith

This all sounds wonderfully liberating, but also a bit remote and abstract. So how do I know if God's grace has acted on me? How do I know if I have been "born again"? The answer to this question is found in 1 Thessalonians 1:4-6:

---

13  Jonathan Edwards beautifully explains this point: "There is a twofold weanedness from the world. One is a having the heart beat off or forced off from the world by affliction, and especially by spiritual distresses and disquietudes of conscience that the world can't quiet; this may be in men, while natural men. The other is a having the heart drawn off by being shown something better, whereby the heart is really turned from it. So in like manner, there is a twofold bringing a man off from his own righteousness: one is a being beat or forced off by convictions of conscience, the other is a being drawn off by the sight of something better, whereby the heart is turned from that way of salvation by our own righteousness. The argument from it being God's manner first to bring persons into extremity, and to take away all false comfort and false dependence, is as forcible for one as the other. . . . In these things, viz. in renouncing the world to trust in Christ only as the means and fountain of our happiness, and in renouncing our own righteousness to trust alone in his righteousness, lies the grand secret of being thorough Christians." *The Miscellanies:* (Entry Nos. 833–1152), ed. Harry S. Stout, Amy Plantinga Pauw, and Perry Miller, vol. 20, *The Works of Jonathan Edwards* (New Haven, CT: Yale University Press, 2002), 90–91.

*For we know, brothers loved by God, that he has
chosen you, because our gospel came to you not
only in word, but also in power and in the Holy
Spirit and with full conviction. You know what
kind of men we proved to be among you for your
sake. And you became imitators of us and of the
Lord, for you received the word in much affliction,
with the joy of the Holy Spirit.*

How does your heart respond to the gospel? Do you
receive the word, no matter the circumstances of
your life? Do you taste the joy of Christ? When our
hearts delight in God, our joy centers on Christ.

The question is simple: Is your heart irresistibly
drawn to the beauty of Christ? Receiving the message of Christ with joy is the essence of saving faith,
and the evidence of God's Joy Project coming alive in
your life.

Joy in Christ, for the sake of Christ, is proof that
God has resurrected our souls and given us new life.
Our supreme joy is no longer in the American dream,
but in the sovereign good. We live in his hope.

Such an incredible joy must be the work of God.
God initiates joy. The place where God chooses to
dwell is a place of joy; the people of God become people of joy.[14] He loves first. If we find our hearts full of
love for God, it is only because the love of God was
set on us in eternity past (1 John 4:19). God's love to
us initiates a new love inside us.[15] In his initiating

14   See Psalms 33:12; 47:1–4; 105:43; 106:4–5; 132:13–16.
15   Jonathan Edwards, *Religious Affections*, ed. John E. Smith and Harry S. Stout, Revised edition,
vol. 2, *The Works of Jonathan Edwards* (New Haven, CT: Yale University Press, 2009), 248–249.

love we discover that our love for God is the effect, not the cause. As one Puritan put it, "We cannot love him till he first loves us. We run because he draws us. We apprehend Christ, but we are first gripped of him."[16]

This is the secret to our happiness. In the words of poet Jackie Hill-Perry: "If pleasure is our aim, then we'll find it when our God is who our target is."[17] This seismic shift in our affections is the work of the divine miracle called *regeneration*.

## Get Happy

The gospel of Jesus Christ is an open invitation into the joys of God—an invitation made dynamic by God's sovereign grace. "It is truly [a] matter of wonder," wrote one man a long time ago, "that the infinitely glorious God should be at so great pains to incline man to pursue his own happiness."[18] Yes, The Joy Project is marvelous in scope and detail. And God does all this for the praise of his eternal glory.

Regeneration substantiates the presence of God's grace. Grace is not theoretical; grace is not abstract. Grace transforms real lives by breaking in and giving us a new taste for something better than anything else. "Grace is God's giving us sovereign joy in God, that triumphs over joy in sin."[19] This is the sure mark of grace.

---

16  Samuel Rutherford, *Fourteen Communion Sermons* (Glasgow: 1877), 254.

17  Jackie Hill-Perry, "The Argument," *The Art of Joy* (2014).

18  Thomas Boston, *The Whole Works of Thomas Boston* (Aberdeen: George and Robert King, 1848) 2:85.

19  John Piper, Twitter, Jan. 5, 2012.

Remember Augustine? He was a sex-addict, and he admitted it. His early adult life was driven by forbidden sexual pleasure, and his heart lusted after glory and wealth. Imprisoned by a love of money and sex, what hope did he have to find true joy? None, really. These sins ruled him, and would have ruined his life. But God acted on him by irresistible grace. Here's what it felt like:

> How sweet did it suddenly seem to me to shrug off those sweet frivolities, and how glad I now was to get rid of them—I who had been loath to let them go! For it was you who cast them out from me, you, our real and all-surpassing sweetness. You cast them out and entered yourself to take their place, you who are lovelier than any pleasure, though not to flesh and blood, more lustrous than any light, yet more inward than is any secret intimacy, loftier than all honor, yet not to those who look for loftiness in themselves. My mind was free at last from the gnawing need to seek advancement and riches, to welter in filth [writhe in mud] and scratch my itching lust.[20]

Augustine paints a stark portrait of sovereign joy in the life of a sinner. This is the tangible fruit of God's incredible plan to destroy pride and despair in his children and to expel the sins of lust and greed by an expulsive joy in Jesus Christ that is stronger, inexpressible, and filled with glory. This is true grace.

20   Augustine, *Confessions*, trans. Maria Boulding (New York: Vintage, 1997), 170.

This is sovereign joy. And God delights to watch this very miracle happen over and over again in the hearts of millions of Christ-loving people on earth throughout the generations.

## Broken Free

So no—no life can shake itself free from the chaos of pride and despair. But in Christ the chains are broken, total depravity routed, and the soul made free by grace. A life freed from the chains of self-glory and from the utter darkness of eternal despair is proof that God has shown up with the Holy Spirit—not confined to an eternity in the grips of the hellishly dark *It* of depression (David Foster Wallace), but to be free forever in the glorious *It* of the sovereign joy of God breaking into our lives (C. S. Lewis).

God planned his Joy Project in eternity, purchased it at the cross, and placed it in the lives of real sinners who were known and chosen by God from eternity past. None of it was accidental. God played it all out in time and history according to divine design. This is how God's Joy Project is applied to lives like ours.

The implications have only begun.

Act 5:

# The Joy Project Unwraps and Unfolds

Only clever detective work could have solved the bathroom shower mystery. Every day, the damp plastic shower curtain in our bathroom was left completely collapsed against one side of the shower. Folded-up curtains, of course, breed mold in the seams and need to be cleaned and replaced more often. Once or twice a day, an open shower curtain is no big deal. My wife would simply close the curtain and move on with her day. The mystery began when the curtain would reopen over and over again, throughout the day, all day long.

So why would the curtain in our main bathroom behave this way? Who was behind it? And why?

My detective wife eventually solved the mystery.[1] The youngest of our children, our seven-year-old son, was found guilty. When he finally confessed his crime, his reasoning was simple and obvious: He is deathly afraid of monsters—monsters in the closet, monsters under the bed, and monsters in the shower. The shower curtain must remain open for him to safely and confidently use the bathroom.

---

1    And not for the first time. Most wives and mothers can piece together events in their house with the most miniscule forensic evidence.

It was a humorous discovery, but enlightening as well. There's a little of my son in me and in all of us. It's part of living in this finite, fragile flesh in this fallen and fearful world. We are haunted people. We are fearing people, and our fears don't end in childhood. It may begin with monsters in the shower, but more disturbing monsters lurk in the shadows as we grow older. We fear athletic and academic failure. We fear star-crossed love or, worse, no love at all. We fear being alone. We fear not getting a good job, or losing our job. We fear losing the health of our children, or losing their affection. We fear that our bills will outgrow our income. We fear job loss, financial hardship, and poverty. As we age, we fear losing our retirement fund, our homes, our minds. Some of our darkest fears can be hedged with insurance, but no insurance will erase every fear. We keep our shower curtains open because we dread the evils that might pounce upon us. It is no mystery that we are more anxious and insecure than we admit.

## Swept Up

All the fears of life set up a beautiful contrast to the security of God's elect. Once God's Joy Project sweeps you into its sovereign security net, it can relieve all fears that some circumstance will befall your life and bring your hope, happiness, and security to an abrupt end. It assures you of joys, now in part, that will only grow more enthralling as they expand into the limitless stretches of God.

This divine drama is the story of how God orchestrated and purchased everything necessary to bless his children forever—all things, for all time, unconditionally. Now, in this final act (of a never-ending story), we can bring all of these acts together into practical application for our lives.

In the context of God's Joy Project, Scripture delivers a whopping promise:

> *What then shall we say to these things? If God is for us, who can be against us? He who did not spare his own Son but gave him up for us all, how will he not also with him graciously give us all things? Who shall bring any charge against God's elect? (Rom. 8:31–33)*

In one glorious passage, we find full proof that God will never let his children fall under condemnation or judgment in Christ. It will never happen, because he gave Christ in the first place. And if God gave up his precious, chosen Son, why would he not provide us, his children, with everything else we need to flourish eternally? He won't hold back. That's the point. "All things" means "all things." His heart doesn't stutter. Everything we need to flourish forever is promised by a gracious heavenly Father eager to bless us lavishly for our joy and for his glory. For his beloved children, the shed blood of Jesus Christ is corroborating evidence to prove that God will stop at nothing to ensure our eternal joy.[2]

---

2   Jonathan Edwards, *Sermons and Discourses, 1734–1738*, ed. M. X. Lesser and Harry S. Stout, vol. 19, *The Works of Jonathan Edwards* (New Haven; London: Yale University Press, 2001), 777–78.

Again it's here in the blood of Christ where all the various threads of The Joy Project converge. Because God gave his only Son for you (limited atonement), he has given you his guarantee that he will weave the details of your life together in such a way as to lead to an eternity with him to enjoy his full pleasures forevermore. To be chosen in Christ is to have the script for your life written, and the end of the story is eternal flourishing.

Of course, the script *includes* conflict and hardships. We don't find joy by escaping this life, but by living it. I don't know how much pain and disappointment you will face, but you will face it. You may face a long season of darkness in depression (as did many of the joy-centered Calvinists quoted in this book). You may live with serious regrets, and those regrets come in many shapes and sizes. Maybe you never intended to be forty and single. Maybe you regret being forty and married. Maybe you regret having kids. Or maybe you regret remaining childless. Or you regret that your child abandoned the faith. Whatever the pains or regrets of life, the happy Calvinist, whose theology has sunk deep into the nerve center of his life, can say: "Though I cannot see why my life has unfolded in the way it has, God is in control and I am upheld by grace." This confidence liberates our hearts to enjoy life. We don't live in self-hate over all our failures. Instead we look back over our lives, knowing that God orchestrated millions of various situations and circumstances and relationships to bring us where we are today.

The apostle Paul, who endured just about every kind of letdown, heartbreak, and suffering imaginable, also acknowledged that his pain was part of God's ultimate plan (2 Cor. 6:3–10). The sorrow he felt was real, and it hurt, but it also proved that the joy of God was inextinguishable. "Our joy no man takes from us," Spurgeon once said. "We are singing pilgrims, though the way be rough. Amid the ashes of our pains live the sparks of our joys, ready to flame up when the breath of the Spirit sweetly blows. Our latent happiness is a choicer heritage than the sinner's riotous glee."[3]

The joy of God in the life of his children is a precious gift, sometimes concealed, but never extinguished by sorrow, conflict, or human circumstances. This is the point of the fifth and final act of God's Joy Project: *perseverance of the saints*, the P of the mnemonic TULIP.

### Joy for Glory

In Christ, God has promised to never leave us or forsake us. No matter what else happens, he guards our souls. The apostle Peter explains this glorious security to fellow sinners who now find themselves caught up into God's sovereign plan of redemption (1 Pet. 1:1–2). To God's foreknown and elect, who are trying to wrap their minds around what has happened to them, Peter explains it like this:

---

3   C. H. Spurgeon, *The Metropolitan Tabernacle Pulpit Sermons*, vol. 28 (London: Passmore & Alabaster, 1882), 187.

*Blessed be the God and Father of our Lord Je-*
*sus Christ! According to his great mercy, he*
*has caused us to be born again to a living hope*
*through the resurrection of Jesus Christ from*
*the dead, to an inheritance that is imperishable,*
*undefiled, and unfading, kept in heaven for you,*
*who by God's power are being guarded through*
*faith for a salvation ready to be revealed in the*
*last time. In this you rejoice, though now for a*
*little while, if necessary, you have been grieved*
*by various trials, so that the tested genuineness*
*of your faith—more precious than gold that per-*
*ishes though it is tested by fire—may be found to*
*result in praise and glory and honor at the reve-*
*lation of Jesus Christ. Though you have not seen*
*him, you love him. Though you do not now see*
*him, you believe in him and rejoice with joy that*
*is inexpressible and filled with glory, obtaining*
*the outcome of your faith, the salvation of your*
*souls. (1 Pet. 1:3–9)*

When it comes to the unspeakable joy God has for
us, this is perhaps the most stunning passage in the
Bible. God's sovereign design stretches out into an
unseen eternal future that awaits us. The passage
walks us through the valleys of darkness and pain
to show us the inevitable: One day we will see Jesus,
and the awesome joy of our hearts in Christ will ignite and burn with a splendid magnificence we can
hardly imagine.

But the plan is not on pause until that day. Already our sin-dead souls have been sparked with

new life in Christ, and we have seen the powers of the world to come: unspeakable glory-joy, the very presence of God! This is worship-filled joy at its highest and fullest. It is joy most authentic. It is a joy full of glory, "infused with heavenly glory and that still possesses the radiance of that glory."[4] It is the joy of God's presence, experienced in the presence of the unseen Christ.

Here are four implications of this passage.

First, God's presence heals our atheistic hearts. The fight club of relational conflicts we studied earlier is solved only when we experience a thirst for more of God, when we humbly draw near to him, and he draws near to us (James 4:1–10).

Second, God's presence is our greatest delight. Puritan Thomas Manton simply comes to a place of expressing his wide-eyed gratitude: "Oh the mutual delights between God and glorified souls!"[5] Yes, they work together.

Third, true happiness is not found. It finds you (1 Pet. 1:1–9). Follow the flow of this passage and it begins with God's sovereign election and ends with our Christ-centered joy. Those two glories are eternally linked in God's plan. Our delight in Christ must follow God's electing grace.

Fourth, God's entire plan from the beginning was that he would be magnified forever by our joy in him. The Joy Project marries God's joy and his glory

---

4   Wayne Grudem, 1 *Peter*, Tyndale New Testament Commentaries (Leicester, UK: Inter-Varsity, 1988), 71.

5   Thomas Manton, *The Complete Works of Thomas Manton* (London: James Nisbet & Co., 1875), 22:132.

to our joy. We delight in God and he delights in us. As we delight in God, God gets the glory. This is not new; it's actually a sweet discovery testified by centuries of careful reading of the Bible. Puritan Richard Sibbes saw it when he wrote: "God is glorified in making us happy, and we enjoying happiness, must glorify God."[6] Puritan David Clarkson wrote:

> The Lord aims at his own glory and our happiness, and we aim at his glory and our happiness. And though he may seem more to seek his glory than our happiness, and we may fear we seek our happiness more than his glory, yet indeed these two are inseparable and almost coincident. That which advances his glory promotes our happiness, and that which makes us most happy makes him most glorious. Wisdom and mercy have made a sweet connection between his honor and our happiness, so that they cannot be disjoined. We need no more fear to come short of happiness than we need to fear that the Lord will come short of his glory, for these two are embarked together.[7]

God's glory is not in competition with our joy. The two are linked, as we will finally explore in the next chapter.

6   Richard Sibbes, *The Complete Works of Richard Sibbes* (Edinburgh, 1862), 1:247.
7   David Clarkson, *The Works of David Clarkson* (Edinburgh, 1864), 3:168.

## Joy Inexpressible

When we come to the end of God's Joy Project, we see that he is moving all of his children toward the beatific vision—a breathtaking moment when we behold the glory of Christ with glorified eyes. This is ultimately where election was leading all along.

Anticipating unending joy in the presence of Christ changes everything. It means we can relinquish control over our lives. It means we have no fear of the future. It means all our pressing toward personal holiness is not in vain. God elects so that we will be conformed to the image of Christ, in his holiness and in his happiness. It will be done, and we strive and obey in this inescapable hope.

First Peter 1:3–9 also teaches us a key lesson about longing and participating. We are not merely left in a subway tube, fiddling on our phones and waiting idly for a tardy train to eventually pick us up and take us to heaven. The Joy Project leads us toward eternal presence with God, but Christ *now* offers us tastes of eternal joy that exceed words.

As Puritan John Owen writes, the physical joys of this life cannot be compared to these precious glimpses of the beatific vision, by faith. "There is no glory, no peace, no joy, no satisfaction in this world, to be compared with what we receive by that weak and imperfect view which we have of the glory of Christ by faith. All the joys of the world are nothing in comparison to what we receive."[8] These "views" are hints of the full beatific vision to come.

8    John Owen, *The Works of John Owen* (Edinburgh: T&T Clark, 1862), 1:415.

But Owen is careful to reiterate these moments are not the everyday state of the Christian life on earth. "There enters *sometimes*, by the word and Spirit, into our hearts such a sense of the uncreated glory of God, shining forth in Christ, as affects and satiates our souls with ineffable joy."[9] These are exquisite moments, but they are infrequent.

Our anticipation for an eternal feast of joy fuels our tastes of present delight (Rom. 5:2). In Christ, we now taste the firstfruits of eternal joy. "As before the sun rises, there are some forerunning beams and streaks of light that usher it in; so the joys of the Holy Spirit are but the morning glances of the daylight of glory, and of the sun of happiness that shall arise upon us in another world."[10]

## Pleasures Forever

For now, we gratefully taste present happiness (periodic joy, by faith) while we eagerly await future happiness (endless joy, by sight). One day this appetizer of spiritual pleasure will give way to the full banquet feast of flooding joys and delights God intends to share with us. This is the climactic finale of God's Joy Project, the end toward which everything is unfailingly headed.

God's Joy Project is pushing all things forward toward a glorious future. No longer will his children live in the past, as strangers and aliens; they will ar-

---

9   Ibid., 1:293. Italics mine.
10   Thomas Manton, *The Complete Works of Thomas Manton* (London: James Nisbet & Co., 1873), 13:331.

rive in the home country to which they have been traveling, to dwell in the presence of God, to live with all the redeemed before the Lamb, clothed in perfect Christlike purity—no spot, no stain, no wrinkle. The Savior will rejoice in receiving us, the ones he's loved from before time; the ones for whom he endured, with joy set before him, the shame of the cross. We will be welcomed into the full enjoyment of his love and it will usher in a joy that will never end or fade.

This is what we anticipate. If we doubt, we look back on the blood of Christ as proof. In the future Christ will feed us abundantly with delights, and he will take us and present us before the Father, who elected us. We will behold God's glory and taste the sweetness of eternal pleasures that we have always desired. All of our sinful longings will finally vanish. All our idols, our pride and despair, our false hopes and securities, our corrupting sins—all these burdens will be burned up like straw in a bonfire. Tears and regret and death will be gone; suffering will be burnt to ash. We will be finally and fully free to enjoy the pleasures of God together.

If you love Christ, hold this promise with firm resolve. You are beloved. God's choice of you is a divine insurance policy of joy, underwritten by Christ's blood, unshaken by the trials and pains of life, ensuring your claim on joys forevermore (Rom. 8:28). Live with the shower curtain closed. Fear not. Only believe that nothing will ultimately get in the way of your perseverance in Christ.

# What Now?

Surrounded by the sights and sounds of their beautiful tulip fields, I'm not sure those Christians in the Netherlands thought of both the acronym TULIP and the experience of joy. But the acronym and the affection work happily together in the world's greatest drama.

The Joy Project began by diagnosing the present course of humanity (T—total depravity), then traveled back in time, before time, into eternity past (U—unconditional election), then jumped forward to the first century (L—limited atonement), returned once again to the present (I—irresistible grace), and then traced out our trajectory into eternity future (P—perseverance of the saints).

We find joy as we discover these truths. Understanding God's sovereignty over all things is intended to ignite our hearts to rejoice.[1] I remember with fondness my early years as a Christian, when I first came to understand God's sovereign plan for my life. It thrilled my soul like nothing I had ever experienced. Never had I felt more loved, more wrapped

---

[1] "Note the ecstatic joy with which God's sovereign rule is proclaimed and praised in (for instance) Psalm 93, 96, 97, 99:1–5, and 103. Men treat God's sovereignty as a theme for controversy, but in Scripture it is matter for worship." J. I. Packer, *Growing in Christ* (Wheaton, IL: Crossway, 1994), 30–31.

up into an eternal purpose, or more confident of my eternal flourishing.

Perhaps for you, God's Joy Project makes immediate sense, and you embrace it and smile. But maybe, for you, coming to see and embrace God's Joy Project has been a struggle—a battle in your heart and mind as it clashes with opposing views. You feel repulsed by The Joy Project, and then confused, yet still drawn in, and then again revolted. Your heart responds like a two-man rip saw, pulling you back and forth between attraction and derision.

Maybe you picked up this book hoping finally to taste and possess the sweet joys your heart desperately longs for, but all the while resisting the doctrines of election and predestination. Maybe the promises of a love like God's are impossible to believe, because you know the searing pain of being unloved, and that sting feels more real to you than the unconditional love of an unseen God.

These inner tensions are natural, and are repeated each time The Joy Project is told to each new generation. We respond with different emotions and at different speeds. But history also reminds us of the great joy to be discovered at the end of theological strivings. It makes the theological pain worthwhile. The midnight black expanse of cloudless heavens will slowly and eventually open up until you discover a sky bejeweled with endless stars—or points of bright, divine initiatives that you never imagined were there. But it may require a long period of patient study and prayer to see the cosmos with such breathtaking clarity. It may take a long time perhaps, and it may feel like a fight. But it's all worth it. In the end, such truth will be increasingly precious because, as one old Calvinist said of his struggle to embrace God's sovereignty, "Truth is no trifle to one who has fought his way to it."[2]

The man who said that last line was nineteenth-century preacher Charles Spurgeon, who emerged from his fight with a true delight in the doctrines themselves. Once he finally embraced God's Joy Project as a deep and personal conviction, it became the soundtrack of his life. "How sweet is the peace which the doctrines of grace will give to the soul; there is nothing like them," he testified. "They are God's sweet lullaby to sing his children to sleep, even in storms. They are God's sheet anchors, which are cast out into the sea, to hold our little vessels fast in the midst of tempests."[3]

Yes. God's Joy Project is the soundtrack behind our unpredictable lives and the anchor of our hopes. "The doctrines of grace are good, but the grace of the doctrines is better still," Spurgeon said.[4] What is most decisive in God's Joy Project is not that we fully grasp it, but that our sovereign God fully grasps us.

But if and when we do embrace it all with firm conviction, God's Joy Project is *felt power* for the raw trials of our lives, and the confidence we need to rest in God's providential care. To know that God has re-

2   C. H. Spurgeon, *The Metropolitan Tabernacle Pulpit Sermons*, vol. 34 (London: Passmore & Alabaster, 1888), 40.
3   C. H. Spurgeon, *The New Park Street Pulpit Sermons*, vol. 2 (London: Passmore & Alabaster, 1856): 203.
4   C. H. Spurgeon, *The Metropolitan Tabernacle Pulpit Sermons*, vol. 25 (London: Passmore & Alabaster, 1879), 633.

solved to bring about our flourishing—and was thus resolved before we were even born—transforms all of life forever.

## What Self-Esteem Never Offers

As we close, I want to pick up a theme I introduced at the beginning of the book. The pursuit of joy is always a dominant force in society, and it always calls for a narrative to make sense of it. Such was the case with a "joy project" authored in 1986, when the California state assembly proposed a State Task Force to Promote Self-Esteem. They inaugurated a social swell that swept across the country, as one writer explained: "Based on the notion that low self-esteem caused every kind of social woe from teenage pregnancy to low test scores and high dropout rates, school curricula and parenting techniques were radically transformed, their main objective now being to cultivate high self-esteem among the young, which activists proclaimed would cure those social woes and make America a safer, happier, and better place. A multibillion-dollar industry surged around self-esteem."[5]

Behind the project was the hope that increasing self-esteem would not only change the climate of American high schools, but would also transform an entire generation and bring wholesale reform to every dark corner of society. Self-esteem, they said, would curb crime, stifle addictions, and boost in-

5   Anneli Rufus, "Low self-esteem is good for you!," *Salon*, May 24, 2014.

tellect. The thought went like this: If everyone feels more secure and certain about themselves, then we will all feel loved, and such a warmth of self-love will ignite a reforming joy throughout society.

To a degree, the premise is right. To be genuinely loved is essential to human flourishing (you'll recall this is what Joelle van Dyne sought in cocaine). But the self-esteem movement failed to deliver. *Saturday Night Live* jumped on the ignorance of the movement with a comedic motivational speaker named Stuart Smalley. His motto—"I'm good enough. I'm smart enough. And doggone it, people like me."— was empty and worthy of all the comedic derision it was intended to get. But it also poked fun at the entire self-esteem movement, which was ultimately about winning the approval of others. And that was the movement's fundamental flaw. The truth is that you will not like me more if I tell you how awesome I am. Such a claim only breeds animosity and distrust. In the end, you're not impressed with me, and I'm not impressed with you. The entire self-esteem project was a failure. The more kids bought into this hallucination of self-superiority, the more they underachieved. The whole self-esteem experiment was later found to lead to a *spike* in bullying, narcissism, elitism, and even racism.

## The Gigantic Secret

The premise behind the self-esteem movement still holds true—in a way. We were made to be happy, which is only possible if we are personally secure and loved.

G. K. Chesterton (1874–1936) profoundly understood this point. He embraced the core importance of joy and used his discovery to debunk false cultural hopes rooted in naturalism and materialism.

One theologian summarized Chesterton's approach as "a novel argument for the existence of God" called "the argument from joy."[6] For Chesterton, the ultimate meaning of joy could be defined in only two ways. Either: (1) Joy is hollow, a mere phantom of a fleeting experience with no ultimate substance behind it and no ultimate meaning under it. Or: (2) Joy is meaningful, so meaningful that joy is found to be the ultimate meaning behind all of created reality.

Either joy is *meaningless*, or joy is *the meaning of the universe*. Chesterton chose the second, and by this discovery his entire theology and worldview came into sharp focus.

Joy is so real and meaningful, it proves the existence of God. "If an argument for God's existence can be based on the phenomenon of joy, then we are in the presence of one of Chesterton's celebrated paradoxes."[7] Yes. Joy is not only real and meaningful, joy calls for the presence of an eternal Joy Giver. In other words, joy proves God.

In Chesterton's understanding of Christianity, the overflowing joy of God is the reason why you and

---

6   Aidan Nichols, *G. K. Chesterton: Theologian* (Manchester, NH: Sophia Institute Press, 2009), 107.

7   Ibid., 116.

I exist right now (more on this in a moment). To exist is to be invited to partake in God's joy. Here's how Chesterton says it, in his own words:

> Man is more himself, man is more manlike, when joy is the fundamental thing in him, and grief the superficial. Melancholy should be an innocent interlude, a tender and fugitive frame of mind; praise should be the permanent pulsation of the soul. Pessimism is at best an emotional half-holiday; joy is the uproarious labor by which all things live. . . .
>
> Christianity satisfies suddenly and perfectly man's ancestral instinct for being the right way up; satisfies it supremely in this; that by its creed joy becomes something gigantic and sadness something special and small. The vault above us is not deaf because the universe is an idiot; the silence is not the heartless silence of an endless and aimless world. Rather the silence around us is a small and pitiful stillness like the prompt stillness in a sick-room. We are perhaps permitted tragedy as a sort of merciful comedy: because the frantic energy of divine things would knock us down like a drunken farce. We can take our own tears more lightly than we could take the tremendous levities of the angels. So we sit perhaps in a starry chamber of silence, while the laughter of the heavens is too loud for us to hear.

> *Joy, which was the small publicity [public in-
> terest] of the pagan, is the gigantic secret of the
> Christian.*[8]

If the heavens lay silent and God seems withdrawn from our lives, it is only because the divine sharing of joy, the frantic energy of divine things, the laughter of the heavens, is too loud for our ears to hear or perceive. Joy is the essence of God's inter-Trinitarian dance of delight, between the Father and the Son, though the Spirit. Joy is divine enthrallment in the Godhead, and it is too much for us.

Chesterton is certainly not trivializing suffering; he is using pain to contrast the power of joy. If in this world, this waiting room of brokenness, God sometimes means for us to feel pain and walk through trials, he also intends that we never stop rejoicing in the midst (2 Cor. 6:10). In its "creed of joy," Scripture reminds us that every tear must be wiped away in the end.[9] God promises a tearless eternity. It will soon appear, and it will prove that joy really was the meaning of the universe after all.

What all this means for us now is that every glimpse of joy, no matter how small, is a panorama of meaning. Joy is the creed of this universe. Joy proves that life is right side up. Joy makes us *feel* the fullness of our humanity before God. Joy is to stand de-veiled and loved and treasured by God. This is what we were made for!

---

8   *The Collected Works of G.K. Chesterton*, vol. 1: *Heretics, Orthodoxy, the Blatchford Controversies* (San Francisco: Ignatius Press, 1986), 364–65.

9   See Isa. 25:8 and Rev. 21:4.

But this happiness does not mean the world feels like a State Fair of endless amusements. No. It means God has taken control of our eternal happiness. Puritan Richard Baxter put it rather bluntly when he wrote: "You are short-sighted and short-witted, and look but to the present relish of things, and choose them if you taste them sweet; but God looks to your everlasting pleasures."[10] This sounds harsh, but it is essentially important for all of us to hear. In reality, this harsh truth is the most loving reality in the universe. We would fumble eternal pleasures every day and replace them with temporal pleasures in this world. But God knows better. He orchestrates our lives—all the pleasures and also all the pains—to guide us toward solid joys forever. He dispenses (and withholds) our present comforts out of a greater concern to preserve our ultimate and eternal happiness.

All of this means The Joy Project fuels our life of joy, in a superior and God-centered way that worldly amusements and self-esteem can never offer. God intends for his children to enjoy his love, and in that love to find the joy that gives life its ultimate meaning.

## The Joy Is Deeper

As anyone who has wrestled with God's sovereignty can tell you, there is great joy in finally discovering that God controls all things for our good. We are

10   Richard Baxter and William Orme, *The Practical Works of the Rev. Richard Baxter*, vol. 10 (London: James Duncan, 1830), 335.

safe. We can rest in the promises of such an awesome God. Yes, and amen. But there is a warning here, too.

Even many Calvinists simply stop here and come up short of the robust beauty of God's Joy Project. The joy of Calvinism is not a joy that hovers around the periphery of the Christian life, waiting until we intellectually comprehend that God is in complete control of everything around us (and in us). The Joy Project goes way deeper than the thrill of discovering God's sovereignty. In the words of Spurgeon, "All the gifts of sovereign grace are intended to give us joy."[11]

Yes, that is the key point: *God gives us joy*. By his own initiative, and by his own inventiveness, and by his own design, which unfolded in Christ, God has sovereignly orchestrated—from the beginning of time—*our joy*. He gives us joy. The triune God—Father, Son, and Holy Spirit—conspired together to fill us with happiness! Now this point gets us to the heart of God's Joy Project.

By all means, discover God's sovereignty and rejoice in the fact that God has control of the universe, governs all evil, and navigates the course of our lives. Grasp this truth from the Bible. But even more, we must see that the Father elected us for joy, the Son purchased joy for us, and the Holy Spirit applies that joy in our lives now and forever. Our triune God promises us a joy that will flourish forever.

In other words, God's Joy Project ensures our joy from two directions. Joy comes out of our hearts,

11   C. H. Spurgeon, *Metropolitan Tabernacle Pulpit Sermons*, vol. 18 (London, 1872), 318.

because God has first put joy *into* our hearts. God's purchased joy is our joy. It may seem redundant at first, but one perfectly good way to say it is this: "Christ-treasuring, blood-bought joy will sustain my joy."[12] That's exactly how the most robust Calvinists should speak of happiness.

## The Cosmic Plan

By now I hope you comprehend one point: The scope of God's Joy Project is as expansive as (indeed more expansive than) the cosmos. It explains why God created the material universe and why he acts out every glorious stage of redemptive history.

First, The Joy Project discloses the mystery of creation. Why did God create this universe, if he had no inherent need for the sun, or for oceans, or for waterfalls—even for us (Acts 17:24–25)? The Joy Project gives us the explanation. Out of his abundant joy, God spun every corner of this vast creation as a place for his children to share in his joy.[13] Creation is the stage designed as the location for God's Joy Project to be acted out in space and time. Chesterton was right all along: Joy explains why the universe exists. The God of eternal joy sought to share his joy with others. Boom! Creation.

More specifically, The Joy Project explains the aim of all redemptive history and sheds light on all of Christ's work, writes Jonathan Edwards.

---

12  John Piper, "Be Constant in Prayer for the Joy of Hope," sermon, December 26, 2004.

13  Jonathan Edwards, *The "Miscellanies"*: (Entry Nos. 501–832), ed. Ava Chamberlain and Harry S. Stout, vol. 18, *The Works of Jonathan Edwards* (New Haven, CT: Yale University Press, 2000), 291.

*The great war that has been maintained between
God and his enemies for the biggest part of six
thousand years has been about one design. . . .
The eternal destruction of God's enemies, both
of devils and wicked men, is in subserviency to
the design of his glorifying himself in his church
in the manner that has been spoken of. He will
glorify his majesty, power and justice before his
elect that they might behold the glory and so be
happy in the sight of this glory of God, and that
they might give God the glory due to him on this
account, and that they might be the more sen-
sible of the worth of their happiness and of the
wonderfulness and sovereignty of God's grace.*[14]

Wait. Slow down, stop, back up, and look at that
quote one more time.

### The Joy Project Centers on God

This magnificent quote from Edwards explains the
purpose of heaven, hell, humans, angels, creation,
and all of redemptive history. God's purpose for creation and redemption is to awaken us to the value
of our happiness and to the magnificence of his redeeming grace.

In other words, God is the main point of The Joy
Project. The story of our joy is the result of a cosmic
storyline in which God chooses to display his mag-

---

14   Jonathan Edwards, "Approaching the End of God's Grand Design," in *Sermons and Discourses,
1743–1758,* ed. Wilson H. Kimnach and Harry S. Stout, vol. 25, *The Works of Jonathan Edwards*
(New Haven, CT: Yale University Press, 2006), 118–19.

nificent glory. Here we finally arrive at the point where we must discover the profound link between God's joy and God's glory—and it means that we need to go deep for a moment.

It gets deep as soon as we realize one profound truth: God's joy is fundamental to his glory (1 Tim. 1:11). And not just any kind of joy. "God's glory consists much in the fact that he is happy beyond our wildest imagination."[15] In other words, essential to God's majesty is a kinetic joy generated as the Father and the Son delight in one another's glory, through the Spirit. This joy-majesty radiates out from the solid-fuel rocket majesty of God's inter-Trinitarian delight. To stand in the presence of God, as his beloved child, is to bask in the highest and purest joy in the universe.[16]

God is the happy King of the universe (1 Tim. 1:11; 6:15). He must be must be essentially happy. He needs nothing. He finds comfort in himself. He is free from evil and filled only with good. He is not only completely happy in himself, he is also the author and source of all true joy for himself and for his creatures to enjoy.[17]

---

15   John Piper, *The Pleasures of God: Meditations on God's Delight in Being God*, Rev. and expanded (Sisters, OR: Multnomah Publishers, 2000), 26.

16   See Matt. 25:23; John 15:11; 17:13.

17   A summary of Richard A. Muller, *Post-Reformation Reformed Dogmatics: The Rise and Development of Reformed Orthodoxy*; Volume 3: *The Divine Essence and Attributes* (Grand Rapids, MI: Baker Academic, 2003), 381–84. Edward Leigh beautifully writes, "The glory of God is internally twofold. Objectively, the glory of God is the excellency of his divine nature, for such is his majesty and excellency, that he is infinitely worthy to be praised, admired, and loved by all. Formally, the glory of God is internal, his own knowledge, love, and delight in himself. For this is infinitely more the glory of God, that he is known and beloved of himself, then that he is loved and praised by all creatures, men or angels, because this argues an infinite worth in God's own nature, that an infinite love and delight is satisfied with it" [Edward Leigh, *A Treatise of Divinity Consisting of Three Bookes* (London: 1646), 2:112].

Reportedly, atheist Friedrich Nietzsche once wrote, "I cannot believe in a God who wants to be praised all the time." Such a statement unmasks a popular distortion about God that simmers under the surface of much unbelief. In reality, God has no need that I can supply. And if God has no need that I can supply, then my worship cannot fill up some dark void of insecurity in him. On the contrary, praise invites my empty soul to be ravished by the beauty of God's glory and to share in the fullness of his eternal joy!

God is not boring. We are boring. Our sinful loves and pleasures are vain, lifeless, and vapid. On the other hand, God's glory is the "frantic energy of divine things" that would now "knock us down like a drunken farce" if our eyes were fully opened. We are too dull and too boring to comprehend the full scope of his joy now.

What all this means is that everything in The Joy Project centers on God's majesty. "God chooses the elect from eternity and for eternity, that he may catch up a beam or a drop of his own blessedness and live as its possessor, that he may rejoice in him and with him." Why? God pours out his joy into us, to go back to himself, "in the service of His self-glorification." That's how it works. We participate as conduits, with God's design that our lives may become "simply gratitude" in return.[18]

But we do not live in isolated, personal worship pods. No, we have been drawn together as God's peo-

---

18   Karl Barth, *Church Dogmatics: The Doctrine of God*, part 2, vol. 2 (London: T&T Clark, 2004), 412–13.

WHAT NOW?                    119

ple (the church). We have been swept up together
into a cosmic plan to participate in God's glory (his
joy), as we magnify the worth of God in our enjoyment of him. Making glad worshipers out of spiri-
tually dead sinners is the grand design of God's Joy
Project. God's glory and our most blissful joy collide
into one end. Our collective joy requires majesty. We
can have no true joy apart from his grandeur. To delight in God's glory is the weightiest matter in the
universe. We were made for this. To behold God's resplendence is to be filled with his holy joy.[19] And as
we are filled with his joy, he is ever more the target
of our praise.[20]

## Simple Gratitude

Simple gratitude. Did you catch that phrase? For all
the lofty words, this simple response sticks so close
to me. It is a small return compared to the magnificent grace I have been given. But in a crazy and dis-
tracting life, its implications are large.

Before the face of God, I feel so insignificant and
flawed. I feel so unworthy of the grace offered to me
in God's Joy Project. On my best days, I still never
rise beyond being just an ordinary guy struggling
to obey God. Perhaps you can relate. The blunt reality is that some days we spend more time checking

19   See Rom. 5:2; 1 Pet. 4:13; Jude 24.
20   See Isa. 60:19–61:3. "The work of God promised to be effected is plainly an accomplishment
of the joy, gladness and happiness of God's people, instead of their mourning and sorrow; and the
end in which the work issues, or that in which God's design in this work is obtained and summed
up, is his glory" [Jonathan Edwards, *Ethical Writings*, ed. Paul Ramsey and John E. Smith, vol. 8,
*The Works of Jonathan Edwards* (New Haven; London: Yale University Press, 1989), 477].

ourselves out in the mirror than focusing on God. We press our faces up close to the glass, examining every feature and every flaw, remembering old scars, and finding new pimples. The sobering reality is that nobody knows our faces like we do, and the more we look in the mirror, the less impressed we get over the years. There are new blemishes to cover every day. Perhaps you look in the mirror only to be reminded that you are heavier than you want to be, not as strong as you used to be, or older than you wish to be. Inside, we feel animosity for what we see in others—the fitness, the trimness, the youth, the beauty, the intelligence—and this envy, however subtle, is just another manifestation of self-loathing. That's life for most of us. These petty concerns eat up so much of our lives, precious time that God wants to redeem with his Joy Project.

And so I go back to *simple gratitude*. In that phrase we can re-center our lives on the cosmic plan of God and return to the sweet joy he is orchestrating. Gratitude doesn't give us easy lives, but it does give us eternal eyes. In the meantime, life will continue to change, season-by-season and moment-by-moment. We will feel high and then low, we will feel loved and then rejected, we will feel thrilled and then depressed, and all because we are wobbling creatures oscillating from one extreme to the other. Yet through all these changes, we can know with certainty that our sovereign, triune God orchestrated his Joy Project over our lives, and this is what gives us confidence, stability, hope, and joy.

## Great Joy Forever

We have come to the end of this incredible story, but we will never come to the end of God's Joy Project. We embrace whatever our finite minds can grasp now, but we anticipate the glory we will hold for all eternity.

God is alive, he is working, he is drawing, and he is "pulling at the other end of the cord, perhaps approaching at an infinite speed, the hunter, king, husband," wrote C. S. Lewis. "There comes a moment when the children who have been playing at burglars hush suddenly: was that a *real* footstep in the hall? There comes a moment when people who have been dabbling in religion ('Man's search for God!') suddenly draw back. Supposing we really found Him? We never meant it to come to *that*! Worse still, supposing He had found us?"[21]

When God breaks into our lives with the beauty of Jesus Christ, we find a true and solid and eternal joy. But of course you and I know better than to say *we found joy*. Rather, *joy found us*—sometimes slowly, sometimes at warp speed. That is the story of TULIP. Calvinism is the story of a long-planned, sovereign joy that finds you before you even see it coming.

In Christ, the title to eternally unending joy is already yours. Christ is yours. Embrace God's Joy Project—designed by the Father, paid for by the Son, applied by the Spirit—as work all accomplished to draw you into the joy of God. Fight your way to embrace this truth with your mind and heart, enjoy it

21  C. S. Lewis, *Miracles: A Preliminary Study* (New York: HarperOne, 2001), 150.

and turn it back to God in praise. Strive to enjoy the foretaste of joy in life now. The day of great joy God has ordained for the future is here, and it's here for you. A day is coming, when the history of this fallen world will be all summed up, and God's glory will be fully manifested before our eyes, and we will see with pristine clarity the entire goal of God's Joy Project—our joy for his glory.

This is why we exist: God created us to participate in his joy—forever! God created us to bask beneath his beams of joy and to magnify him in worship. God created us to stand before him, thrilled with joy, in praise of Christ forever. We strive to live this truth out now, by faith.

Once we see that God's glory was the aim all along, then his sovereignty and our joy come together. Our lives are brightened with the light of one glorious closing benediction:

> Now to him who is able to keep you from stumbling and to present you blameless before the presence of his glory with great joy, to the only God, our Savior, through Jesus Christ our Lord, be glory, majesty, dominion, and authority, before all time and now and forever. Amen. (Jude 24–25)

# Thanks

This little book exists because John Piper has invested into my life—challenging me to become a better writer, exegete, and theologian. He is resolved to multiply a new generation of writers at desiringGod.org who revel in the beauty of Christ and who labor to articulate this beauty in fresh ways. To this end he pushes us forward through private correction and public applause. More specifically related to this book project, I thank Pastor John for one seminal paragraph he wrote in his biographical message on Augustine (cited on page 6), a seed that germinated in my mind and branched out and became this book over time.

It is hard to find words to express my gratitude for the staff at desiringgod.org. I am one voice, surrounded by a chorus of remarkably gifted creatives, all clustered together in a Minneapolis office working, learning, and growing. The DG content team is not the Inklings, but it is the closest thing I will likely ever experience to it—in male laughter, friendship, likeminded gospel labor, and in pushing one another to creative and writing excellence.

Our team at desiringGod.org is empowered to pioneer online because we have generous and joyful financial donors at our back! To publish this book online, free of charge to the world, is the fulfillment of a personal dream, and it could never happen without the precious friends who support desiringGod.org.[1] To each of you who support our work, I dedicate this book. As you hold it in your hands, I pray it becomes one tangible token of the many hundreds of new resources we create each year and share online free of charge to the world, made possible by your support.

And finally, thanks to my team of editors, which included my friend Jon Vickery, a sharp historian, theologian, and wordsman who helped me better explain Puritan psychology, honed my metaphors, and straightened my prose. My friend Paul Maxwell stepped in to buff out a few of the dull bits. Lydia Brownback worked her magic to edit and format the entire manuscript. David Mathis carved out time to put his keen editing eyes on it, too. In the end, my friend Bryan DeWire combd the book with his ealge eye to clean up typsos (oops—missed some!). He's used to my abuse.

Of course none of my books escape into the world without the input of Karalee, my rib, my best friend, my editoress, whose creative excellence shaped and sharpened every sentence in this book.

Yes, it really takes all these people to make me readable. Any remaining errors or confusions in these pages are the product of a small mind trying to make sense of eternal profundities.

1   Download this book in three digital formats, free of charge, at desiringGod.org.